In this book "from the field," Kathryn Kirigin and Carol Warren give us an unstinting look at older women's experience with their bodies—in all the particulars. The authors raise provocative questions: Are we or are we not our bodies? How much intervention is appropriate to keep up appearances? Readers will find fresh reflections on how to conduct oneself across time, and the advice to "carry on…inside and despite our bodies."

David J. Ekerdt, *Professor of Sociology and Gerontology, University of Kansas, and President of the Gerontological Society of America*

The book is a real contribution, an extraordinary book that amasses important historical and contemporary information not easily found. The authors deserve applause for their scholarship, their fearlessness and personal vulnerability, and their unflinching attention to the truth of aging bodies and minds. It should be valuable for courses in human sexualities, gerontology, nursing, social work, sociology and gender studies.

Pepper Schwartz, *University of Washington—Seattle*

OUR BODIES NOT OURSELVES

In 1970, the best-seller *Our Bodies Ourselves* was published. The focus of the authors, the Boston Health Collective, was on the youthful female body: on reproduction, sexuality, genitalia, intimacy and relationships in the context of North American cultural expectations. *Our Bodies Not Ourselves* is also about the female body—but on women aging from menopause to 100. Like its predecessor, *Our Bodies Not Ourselves* covers sexuality, genitalia, intimacy, gender norms and relationships. But the aging woman's body has many other issues, from head to toe, from skeleton to skin, and from sleep to motion.

The book, an ethnography and Western cultural history of aging and gender, draws upon history, culture and social media, the authors' own experiences as women of 70, and conversations and correspondence with more than two hundred women aged from 60-ish to 100. They consider the cultural and structural frameworks for contemporary aging: the long sweep of history, gendered cultural norms and the vast commercial and medical marketplaces for maintaining and altering the aging body. Part I, The Private Body, focuses on the embodied experiences of aging within our private households. Part II, The Public Body, explores weight, height, and adornment as old women appear among others. Part III, The Body With Others, sets the embodied experiences of aging women within their sexual and social relationships.

Kathryn A. Kirigin is Professor Emerita at the University of Kansas, USA. Her writing has appeared in the *Journal of Organizational Behavior Management* and the *Journal of Applied Behavior Analysis*, among others.

Carol A.B. Warren is Professor Emerita at the University of Kansas, USA. She is the author of ten books, most recently *The Lotos Eaters: Aging and Identity in a Yacht Club Community* (Routledge, 2016), and nearly fifty articles, papers and reviews.

OUR BODIES NOT OURSELVES

Women Aging from Menopause to One Hundred

Kathryn A. Kirigin
Carol A.B. Warren

NEW YORK AND LONDON

First published 2019
by Routledge
711 Third Avenue, New York, NY 10017

and by Routledge
2 Park Square, Milton Park, Abingdon, Oxon, OX14 4RN

Routledge is an imprint of the Taylor & Francis Group, an informa business

Library of Congress Cataloging-in-Publication Data
A catalog record for this book has been requested

ISBN: 978-1-138-60237-3 (hbk)
ISBN: 978-1-138-60238-0 (pbk)
ISBN: 978-0-429-46960-2 (ebk)

Typeset in Caslon Pro
by Apex CoVantage, LLC

We dedicate this book to our mothers, Peggy and Mabs.
We never knew.

Contents

Acknowledgments

We are deeply indebted to our publisher, Dean Birkenkamp, his assistant, Tyler Bay, and to Derek Brahney, who permitted us to use his brilliant photograph for our cover. We want to thank the anonymous reviewers of *Our Bodies Not Ourselves* and the friends and colleagues who read various drafts and made suggestions; above all Shirley Hill, our sister from another mother. We celebrate the women and men whose voices are heard in this book; without you, this would never have happened. We are delighted with our next generations: Kathi's daughter and son-in-law, Regan and Kent Broadfoot, and her grandson, Bob; her son, Robert Ramp; and Carol's son and daughter-in-law, Ian and Teija Staples. And we have each other as we grow old, for which we are profoundly grateful.

PREFACE

Our Bodies Not Ourselves

In 1970, the Boston Women's Health Collective published *Our Bodies Ourselves*. In it, women writers claimed their bodies for themselves, unshackled from culture, technology, the marketplace and relationships. They explored and reveled in female sexuality and bodily passion. We, the authors of *Our Bodies Not Ourselves*, were in our early twenties then, at a time in history when there was still some shame and mystery attached to female flesh. Menstruation was "the Curse," and masturbation was something men did—and it might drive them blind or mad. But 1970 was also a time when we could lay claim to ourselves, and *Our Bodies Ourselves* helped us learn to enjoy our bodies and be unafraid. Although our culture encouraged dependence upon fathers and husbands, we could escape that bondage if we wished. Or, together with the men in our lives, we could rewrite the terms of engagement.

In the decades since 1970, we have become mature, then middle aged, and—now—old. Our bodies, claimed as our own in our youth, no longer seem like ourselves. We look in the mirror and see not ourselves looking back, but our mothers—even our grandmothers. We look at our hands and wonder where all those spots came from, and the crooks in our fingers, and the wrinkles in our cheeks. *Our Bodies Not Ourselves: Women Aging from Menopause to One Hundred* takes the story of women's bodies after menopause, into our sixties, seventies, eighties and nineties—and even into and beyond 100: a memoir and ethnography of we women and our old bodies.

From menopause to 100 is a long journey: from middle age to advanced old age. Among old women, as for most people, there is a considerable contrast among these later stages of life. The relative fitness and sociability of "early" old age nowadays often extends through people's sixties and seventies, even into their early eighties, at least for those with adequate means of support and access to good health care. However, "increasing debilities . . . become harder to avoid as people reach their mid-eighties" (Segal, 2013: 225). The march of time is not without its own music, even for those of us who are privileged.

For most women in the United States, menopause occurs by the time we turn 60. Many women in their sixties do not feel old; we certainly did not. Around 60, we were middle aged—but not that far from youthfulness. We spent hours on the beach, in the water, walking, on the tennis court; our skin tanned and our (admittedly dyed) hair bleached by the sun. We were endlessly on the move. We did not notice the enormity of the difference between youth and old age that we now do. But we did recognize that some 60-year-old bodies were showing serious wear. Louise, 63, has had a knee and a hip replacement and had to give up her athletic pursuits more than a decade ago. Laura, 65, has had heart trouble, and her face bears the wrinkles of years in the sun.

But for many of us, 70 is the starting gate of old age. The number itself is daunting (whoever said that age is just a number should remove the word "just" from that phrase). Meredith, 87, says that: "turning seventy sounds old. I never referred to myself as old before then." Lee, 87: "I did not begin to feel old until I turned seventy." And it is not JUST the number. Kitty, 70, speaks for many of us when she says, "I did everything at sixty. Now I can hardly get through the day." And as Kathi says: "At sixty, I was not constantly aware of the imminent end of things." For a few others, turning 80 is the onset of old. As her 80th birthday approaches, Lynn says, "I am old, I am ugly, and I can't do anything." Yet there are a few 80-year-olds who contend that they do not feel old; Eve, 82, speaks of "old people" as if they come from another country. People in their nineties are among the oldest old—but they may or may not concur. Norma's hair expresses her view of aging; she colored it blond until her mid-eighties, then let it grow out to white. When we saw her again in her nineties, she had resumed being a blonde. Mac went dancing with his wife Alice every Friday night while he was in his early nineties, and they went to the gym three times a week. Ella, 90, stumbles and falls quite frequently, but she will not use a cane because it makes her look old. She says, "No, no, I know how to fall." And, indeed, there are classes that teach people how to fall without hurting themselves as much as they might have otherwise.

Several of the 90-year-olds we knew when we began to write this book have died. We know of, but do not know, women past their nineties. We used to see one woman of 100 being wheeled around the streets where we live by her 80-year-old daughter. Indirectly, we know of several who have reached 100 years from the comments about them from of their 70- and 80-year-old children. Most of these centenarians are in nursing homes, relying on whatever resources they have garnered during a lifetime, and sometimes the resources of the younger generations as well. At least one old woman whose 92-year-old mother was living at home with expensive round the clock caregivers expressed a fervent wish that her parent get on with dying. Sylvia, at 67, spoke of her mother: "Surely she won't last past February!" The mother actually lasted for two years past the next February, and Sylvia died soon after her.

We were all young once. In our youth many of us embodied the body ideal: straight, slender, upright body; white teeth; unblemished skin; taut, firm breasts, abundant hair on the head, underarms and pubis; shell-like finger and toenails; straight hands and feet, clear sight, hearing, and taste, sweet smell. Old age is: stooped body; teeth that are gray, brown or missing; spotted skin; drooping breasts, thin, gray or missing hair, and hair in the wrong places; thick yellow finger- and toenails; bunions, hammertoes and arthritis; fading sight, hearing and taste. Our youthful bodies walk and run with grace, while our old bodies are slow as snails. In youth our bodies were in varied relationship to the ideal, but the aging body is for all of us: women, men, the wealthy and the poor, the obese and the disfigured.

Our Bodies Not Ourselves is an ethnography and memoir, encompassing the experiences of about 200 old women. Two-thirds of them are our neighbors in Southern California, while the others are friends, relatives and former colleagues around the country. We have known some of them for a few months, others for fifteen or thirty years. Although most of the women are aged 60 to 90; there are a few younger women's voices, and a few men's and young women's, also. We use pseudonyms for these women, their partners or husbands and their friends and family. We use the term "old women," rather than euphemisms such as "senior citizen" or "elderly" throughout the book. This is not only our preferred term, it is also the preference of most of the old women we spoke to. As Ruby, 80, said, "For God's sake just call us what we are, old women. I hate to be called elderly. Or a senior citizen."

Although old, the women we know are resilient, having survived the deaths of loved ones and encounters with cancer and heart disease. They are also privileged, with at least an adequate income and medical care. The majority live in their own homes, although a few people in their nineties have moved to independent or assisted living facilities. And they are in vibrant social circles. Most of the women have current spouses or partners; many of them are veterans of up to five marriages. A few remain widowed or divorced. Some are married to older men, others to slightly younger men; quite a few have married the same spouse twice. They have grandchildren and great-grandchildren. Some belong to a church, others to the local yacht club, country club or golf club. They travel all over the country and the world, as long and often as they can.

Other ethnographies of the old at home and in communities have documented a similar resilience, even among less well-off elders. Barbara Myerhoff's classic *Number Our Days* (1979) explores survival among old, poor Orthodox Jews in a Jewish neighborhood and community center; she describes their existence as "triumphant." This theme been echoed in subsequent ethnographies, such as Meika Loe's (2011) study of thirty people—from poor to affluent—aged 85 to 100—in New York State. Loe, like Myerhoff, celebrates the oldest old as vibrant and resilient, although with the inevitability of decline and death not too far away.

In these ethnographies, as in ours, the aging body tests us with its inadequacy, discomfort or pain; as Loe (2011: 28) comments, old people face not only ageism and financial issues but also "chronic health issues . . . [and] an acute sense of mortality and loss." For the women in our ethnography, there is ageism, but rarely are there financial issues. There are chronic health issues, loss and the fear of death. Throughout this aging process, the woman's body changes both cosmetically and functionally. And the body we see is no longer the body that we delighted in when we were in our twenties; it seems that it is our Body, but it is not our Self; it is an interloper that has taken us over and does not represent what we look like, or used to look like, or want to look like. Thus, for those of us who are in our sixties and beyond—it is *Our Bodies Not Ourselves* (2005).

We speak with our own voices as well as those of the women we know. As other feminist writers have noted (Hurd, 2010; Holstein, 2015), women do not begin to contemplate old age, either in their own lives or as research topics, until they themselves begin to experience the wrinkles and the graying hair that signal the beginning of the end of youth. Hurd describes the conflicting feelings she experienced as she wrote about facing age: "anxiety, wonder, incredulity, admiration, despair, hilarity, hope, compassion, revulsion, resilience, denial, sadness, and fear" (2010: 2). Talking with aging women is combined with what Simone de Beauvoir (1972) calls the "existential . . . being in the world" of the aging woman scholar.

Both Simone de Beauvoir and Betty Friedan, as they aged, took on aging as a topic. De Beauvoir's book on men's and women's aging (1972) uses mostly literary, philosophical, historical and comparative examples, but she also turns her lens on herself. "When I was only forty I still could not believe it when I stood there in front of the looking glass and said to myself, 'I am forty'" (p. 283). And the eternal question of the old women: "'Can I have become a different being while I still remain myself?'" Betty Friedan, in *The Fountain of Age* (1993), made aging into an academic project, interviewing aging men and women. But she begins her book with her own experiences: "When my friends threw a surprise party on my sixtieth birthday, I could have killed them all" (p. 13). Like de Beauvoir, Betty Friedan moved reluctantly through middle and into old age; also (somewhat) like de Beauvoir, she concludes her book with a triumphalist view of age as a creative fountain. Her own body, as well as interviews with others, is an occasional witness to aging. When told she needed cataract surgery, she rebelled:

> How in all honesty could I go on speculating about the fountain of age when I was losing my own eyesight? . . . And I wasn't even sixty-five! . . . [but] when the doctor took the bandage off, the day after the lens implant, I saw more clearly than I had in years. Medical advances like the lens implant were surely part of the fountain of age.
>
> (p. 28)

We the authors were shaped by the changes in gender roles and marital expectations that occurred between the 1950s and subsequent decades . . . during the years that feminist scholarship took root and developed. We came of age in the 1960s, when women's voices began to be heard collectively, at least the privileged voices of the college educated. Our book's title is based on, and is in homage to, *Our Bodies Ourselves*, which has gone through numerous editions and been published in many countries and languages. We each, in our separate worlds and lives, bought copies of the book, although we both lost track of them during later decades.

Our Bodies Ourselves focused on the reproductive and sexual aspects of women's bodies as they grew up, matured, menstruated, reproduced, used contraception and underwent abortion and menopause in the company of their husbands, lovers and children. For we, the old women, menstruation, reproduction, contraception or abortion are in our bodies' past, although issues of sexual relationships and marriage domination or equality may remain. But the body insists, from the seventieth decade if not before, that it has many other parts and problems than the reproductive and sexual. Feet hurt and grow knobs; so do fingers. Hair thins. Teeth fall out. Digestive systems rumble and fail. Backs and shoulders bow. Muscles wither. When we lift our arms, skin folds and sags. So, in our version of *Our Bodies*, it is the entire body and its parts to which we attend.

Our experiences of aging are not only local and relational, they are also structural and cultural. Twigg and Martin (2015) focus on ageism:

the ways in which everyday life, economic arrangements and the nexus of appearance, identity and consumption combine to disadvantage the old as against the young adult. There is a structural politics of ageism and an ageist politics of everyday life. Factors such as eldercare, the marketplace and sexual and social relationships surround old women's bodies with a series of dilemmas: is it less expensive to go into assisted living or stay at home with home help? Should I get long-term care insurance? Dye my hair? Register with a dating service? Our answers to these questions shape our embodied selves.

We learned about old bodies from ourselves, from the old women who spoke and wrote to us, from dealing with Medicare and pension plans, and from the voices and images of old—and young—women as they appear in print and on the internet from fashion magazines to social media tweets and blogs. We examine images and text as well as firsthand experience to illustrate our discussion of the old woman's body in the context of contemporary and culture marketplace, and to fill in the gaps in our firsthand knowledge. There are some topics, such as marital sex or the onset of dementia, that we cannot ask about and that the old women rarely talk about—except jokingly. So we turn to published accounts, such as Geri Taylor's on Alzheimer's (Kleinfield, 2016) and blogs about sex such as www.dailymailco.com.

There are limits to what we discuss. There is a line—albeit wiggly—between the everyday issues of aging and the diagnostic and treatment possibilities of medicine. Any one of the body issues we discuss—lesions on the skin, for example—can become the object of medical diagnosis and treatment, layering the implications of, say, "skin cancer" over those of "age spots." We are not qualified to work with medical diagnoses and treatments. But there are some conditions and experiences among the old women whose medical labels are commonplace: arthritis, osteoporosis, senile pruritis, dementia, hip replacements, knee replacements. We, the old women, speak of these within the fabric of our everyday lives.

There are also autoimmune conditions that mimic or accompany aging, so that we learn not to attribute everything to the process of growing older. Fawn, 62, was diagnosed with multiple sclerosis in her forties and since then has had strokes and seizures. As she ages, the pains of MS accompany those of growing older. Clarice, 82, developed an enormous red and black sore on her calf and spent months in a search for a diagnosis and treatment—is it cancer? MRSA? A brown recluse spider bite? Perhaps an autoimmune disorder? Clarice has gone to generalists and specialists, with as yet no answer. As we grow older, we learn about more and more conditions and afflictions with names, and we learn more about those that as yet have no name.

People 65 and older are covered for some medical conditions and treatments by Medicare; those with additional resources may purchase additional coverage privately. Bodily problems of the old—or the young—can take them to the hospital ER or admitting suite. As of this writing, there is a problem for hospitalized old people. A national news program alerted us to this problem early in 2017; within a few months, two of the old women we know had encountered it. Ruby, 80, writes of her 90-year-old husband

> He has cancer and a broken back after a fall. He was admitted to the hospital on "observational" rather than "admitted" status. I just learned that this means Medicare will not pay for the PT or other things that he needs. I have been talking with hospital staff to remedy this, but it has not been remedied. Once he leaves the trauma center and goes to a regular ward under observational status, Medicare won't pay for his hospitalization.

Ruby has amassed an army of lawyers and elder advocates to fight the system—as have many other individuals and organization. She can afford it, and she knows that it is a problem. Other old people, including some featured on national news programs, do not have advocates and do not know why they are getting enormous hospital bills.

Even though all women are on Medicare, we cannot speak for all women. The poor, intersex or transgender people, or women of color have problems of embodiment, health and wealth different from ours. We hope that others will explore further the aging bodily experiences of minorities and the poor, and of men and transgender people as well as women. Although both Simone de Beauvoir and Betty Friedan wrote about aging men as well as women, we did not include them in our ethnography. Although the men we know may talk to their wives and other women about their bodies, they most certainly do not talk to us.

We live in our bodies, among others, in cultures and within a global capitalist marketplace. Throughout the book, we note the possibilities for the making as well as the spending of money on the aged body, as cohorts of the aging swell the population. Some of these possibilities are products for the external body, such as face cream, hair dye and nail polish. Others are to be purchased and then ingested: "graying" vitamin supplements, anti-aging liquids and pills, and laxatives. Workers and workplaces are involved, too; from the personal trainer specializing in old women's bodies to the hair salon to international companies that manufacture "beauty care" and advertise in the media. There are researchers in these companies whose business it is to "prove" the safety and efficacy of the products, others to make and others to sell the product. Crossing over the line of medicalization are the hospitals, surgeons, dermatologists and others who perform bariatric surgery, face-lifts or skin abrasion. We mention many of these marketing opportunities in our discussion of the aging body, but to mention them all would fill an encyclopedia—and we want to avoid product placement.

There are medical interventions into the aging body, and there are also cosmetic ones. The most radical of body businesses is the cosmetic surgery industry, which purports to alter, shape, and lift the body, from head to toe. The American Society for Plastic Surgery (www.plasticsurgery. org) claims that in 2015 there were 15.9 million "minimally invasive and surgical" cosmetic procedures performed in the United States, up by 2% from the previous year. The American Society for Aesthetic Plastic Surgery says that in 2015, 13.5 billion dollars were spent on cosmetic procedures (www.surgery.org). Not all plastic surgery is performed on women (men have, for example, breast reductions) or on old people (younger people have breast augmentation and nose jobs). But the aging female body is a prime target for intervention, from head to toe. Whatever the objections of young and older feminists to cosmetic age defiance (Holstein, 2015), it has taken root in our culture and our worlds (Brooks, 2017). Although there are other marketplaces for changing the body cosmetically, such as hair dye or face creams, it is plastic surgery that epitomizes women's repudiation of their aging bodies.

The why of the success of the marketplace in persuading women to change their bodies cosmetically can be found in Western culture, which privileges young over old bodies and men's over women's. We begin our narrative of the body with the amply-documented history of the aging female body in Western culture; the ways it has been represented in narrative and image. We consider the contemporary representation of the aging female body in books, movies, TV and social media. This introductory chapter forms the historical and cultural background to subsequent chapters on the private body, the public body and the body with others.

1
THE AGING BODY FROM PAST TO PRESENT

Historians, philosophers and cultural critics have written about aging and the aged since the Greeks and Romans (and the Egyptians before them). In this our Western heritage, youth and vitality were prized over old age, except, perhaps, in governance. Williams (2017) notes that "The ancient Greeks generally abhorred aging, as it represents a decline from highly prized youth and vigor." In the seventh century BCE Sparta instituted the Gerontocomia, a governing body consisting of men over 60 years of age. The Romans continued to prize bodily youth but permitted old men to govern. Cicero, who also noted that old men were useful in governance, said, around 40 BCE, that "What I find most lamentable about old age is that one feels that one is repulsive to the young." Within this Western tradition, old women were of no use past childbearing age. But at the same time, the theory of the gendered body was more fluid than it is today.

For centuries, bodies were seen as the same gender; women were the same as men but turned inside-out. But this turning-in or out made all the difference in social status and power. Men wore pants and ruled the kingdom and the household; women bore and raised children. A man could not turn into a woman, but a woman could turn into a man—the male genitals inside her dropping down. As late as the early 1950s, Carol's mother warned her not to run around too much, or she would turn into a man—the male genitals hidden inside her body would pop out. No such luck; she ran around in the full knowledge that the externality of genitals would bring about all kinds of wondrous social changes, most surrounding the notion of being the first, the most, the important, the best, the kings. All that women had, in the folklore of British women of Carol's mother's age, was a set of genitals they described as "tidier and nicer" than men's. The parts of those genitals, such as the clitoris (the "man in the boat") were, like children, neither seen nor heard about. Although women's genitals were to be guarded by chastity belts or cultural norms, women's bodies were of far less importance than men's.

The "Ages of Man" have been celebrated (at least the early stages of youth) by centuries of scholars and poets and investigated by centuries of scientists. What causes "Man" to age and die, and is the process natural, inevitable, or unnatural and stoppable? Astrology, the humors, God, the environment, medical care or its lack, heredity and the habits of the heart and body have all been invoked at one time or another. Cryogenics preserve our body for rebirth into an unknown future, while cloning duplicates the body like a sort of rubber stamp. Scientists follow the super-old with the utmost fascination, and so do we.

The differences in aging between women and men have had various explanations, none of them particularly flattering to women. Throughout most of Western history, fewer women than men survived into old age because of problems associated with childbirth. But women who reached the age of 40 were likely to live longer than men who reached 40 (Minois, 1989; Russell, 1990). One explanation for women's longer lifespan was their inactivity relative to men. If the bodily heat is a constant, and the process of aging involves cooling down and drying out, then women will live longer than men because they move around less (Bacon, [1638] 1903: 127).

While old women and men may (or may not) be wiser, more temperate, more self-controlled and more spiritual, they are not likely to be more beautiful or handsome than the young. Bodily decline has been lampooned throughout the ages. In the seventeenth century, Sir Francis Bacon paints a word portrait of an old man who is

> dry skinn'd and impudent, hard bowell'd and unmercifull; bleare ey'd, and envious; downlooking, and stooping . . . trembling limbs,

wavering, and unconstant, crooked finger'd, greedy and covetous, knee trembling, and fearfull, wrinkled and crafty.

(Bacon, 1638: 279)

Women fared worse than men, their bodily decline the object either of fear or of sexual disgust. Myth and folklore give us "terrifying images . . . hag, harridan, witch, Medusa" (Segal, 2013). Around the first century CE, an epigram described a woman called Timo whose

back is bent like a yard-arm lowered, and your grey fore-stays are slack, and your relaxed breasts are like flapping sails, and the belly of your ship is full of bilge-water and her joints are shaky. Unhappy he who has to sail still alive across the lake of Acheron on this old coffin-galley.

(Wortley, 1996: 5)

Sexuality, in Western culture, is the provenance of the young; for women, this meant of menstruating and childbearing age—not old and full of bilgewater like Timo. For the ancients, menstrual blood was toxic, and the function of menstruation was to eliminate poisonous humors. With the cessation of menstruation, the woman became "a repository of poison" (Rawcliffe, 1995: 175). Although sex with young women was widely seen, in premodern times, as an antidote to old age for men, copulation between a young man and an older woman, although similarly beneficial to the woman, was likely to be fatal to the man:

To see a woman advanced in age grow not only brisk and lively but strong and healthy, by marrying a young husband? She drinks his breath, exhales his spirts, extracts his moisture, and invigorates herself, while the poor man, suffering from the impure contagion of her sinks very quickly into an apparent weakness—and falls at last into what the common people call a galloping consumption. Strange! That the death of a young man should result from his marriage with an old woman, and that the taking of a young wife should repair the waste, and prolong the life, of an old man. Yet so it is.

(Cohausen, 1771: 1089–1090)

Old women are criticized by men (old and young) for the deterioration of their bodies, for their interest in sex and marriage with men, and for attempting to alter their bodies by cosmetic procedures. There is historical evidence that women in ancient Greece devised strategies to appear more youthful, including hair dye, hair pieces, lead-based makeup, and eyebrow tweezing (Richardson, 1933: 11). In the first century CE, Antiphilus of Byzantium complains about makeup, hair dye and heat-based hair curlers:

Even if you smooth the skin of your many-trenched cheeks and blacken with coal your lidless eyes and dye your white hair black and hang around your temples curly ringlets crisped by fire this is useless and ridiculous.

(Wortley, 1996: 7)

Erasmus, in the sixteenth century, mocks the sexuality and cosmetic strategies of old women:

It is . . . fun to see the old women who can scarcely carry their weight of years and look like corpses that seem to have risen from the dead. They still go around . . . on heat "longing for a mate" . . . They're forever smearing their faces with make-up and taking tweezers to their pubic hairs . . . trying to rouse failing desire . . . absolute foolishness.

(quoted in Minois, 1989: 255–256)

Modern feminist scholars sometimes agree. Germaine Greer (1992: 13) says that women after menopause range from those, like Greer herself, who have lost all interest in sex, to those who—like a much-criticized friend whom she quotes extensively—are "enslaved by sex."

Although some geriatric specialists cautioned old men against having sex (Zerbi, 1489), other writers applauded men who did so. Thomas

Parr, an Englishman who was reputed to have been born in 1483 and lived until 1635, was saluted in a long poem both for his first marriage at 80 and (disguised as a reprimand) his adultery at 105. Men who wanted to but could not achieve an erection lamented their bodily weakness. Maximianus wrote a "dirge" for his "Pecker" around 550 CE when he became impotent with a Greek cabaret performer. He concludes that "Although my member is dead I shall live in my art" (1988: 335–336).

There were a few male and female exceptions to the bodily problems of aging. At the age of 81, the Italian sixteenth-century self-help author Luigi Cornaro wrote that he was healthy, agile, strong and vigorous— without directly mentioning his Pecker. In the eleventh century, an author wrote about a woman called Charito, who was sexually attractive in her sixties:

> Still the mass of her dark hair is as it was, and still upheld by no encircling band those marble cones of her bosom stand firm. Still her skin without a wrinkle distils ambrosia, distils fascination and ten thousand graces. Ye lovers who shrink not from fierce desire, come hither, unmindful of her decades.
>
> (Wortley, 1996: 10)

Many decades later, and in a different time and place, Benjamin Franklin (1745) recommended that young men should have sex with older women not because of their youthful bodily beauty but for the state of their genitals:

> The Face first grows lank and wrinkled; then the Neck; then the Breast and Arms; the lower Parts continuing to the last as plump as ever.

In addition, "in the dark all Cats are grey," and the old women not only "learn to do 1000 services small and great" they "are so grateful!"

But why does it have to happen, this aging of the body? The process of aging and death has been the subject of inquiry in Western culture from the time of the Greeks. There have been four general explanations, by experts, for aging and the miseries of the edifice: the humors, God's punishment, a natural process or a set of medical problems that can be cured. The theory of the humors proposed that bodies have a certain amount of heat, which is dissipated over a lifetime until the coldness of the flesh signifies death. Heat is dissipated by activity, so that women who did not die of childbirth complications lived longer than men because they moved around less.

Premodern Christian clerics believed that there had been a shortening of the human lifespan since the Biblical patriarchs: "Before the Flood, as the sacred Scriptures declare, men lived a hundred years" (Bacon, 1638). Things went from bad to worse, from generation to generation; in the hands of an infuriated God, Shem died aged 600, Abraham at 175 and Plato at 81. There are few among the old women who see their aging as God's punishment, but there are adopters of the natural and medical approaches—and the cosmetic, scorned by the ancients (men).

The "natural" theory of old age posits the inevitability of death together with the prolongation of a healthy life through environmental possibilities and individual choices. Modern geriatrics and gerontology were foreshadowed from Greek and Roman into medieval times by specialists called "gerontocomos." One of them, Zerbi (1489), who argued for the biomedical treatment of old age, quoted Aristotle on the relationship between astrology, the humors and the humoral composition of the body:

> Aristotle says that the time and life of each man has its number and . . . it is determined that the revolutions of the heavens . . . the extension of life, the period and limit of each living creature are determined by the kind of complexion which is contained in the individual.
>
> (Zerbi, [1489] 1988: 723)

Only "man's" aging was relevant to Zerbi. He designed an assisted living facility (the "gerontocomia") for old men and claimed that women were only useful for raising chickens (Warren, 2012).

Some premodern geriatric experts proposed lifestyle modifications as the basis of staving off the depredations of the aging body, especially moderation in all things—a catchword that has echoed through the decades despite detachment from the mother-theory of the balancing of the humors. Arnaldus of Villa Nova wrote a 1290 handbook on aging, said by his translator Jonas Drummond to have gone through 240 editions between 1475 and 1845, in which he recommends "moderation inn all things" for old people. More than 200 years later, Cornaro stressed temperance. Leonard Lessius, in the eighteenth century, blamed intemperance on society's increasing "luxury," the consequence of which was poor diet and damaged nerves and muscles (1743: 18).

Although the gerontocomos were interested in the stars as a source of the fate of the aging body, some of them also looked at the environment. Zerbi (1489) gave specific and careful advice as to where an assisted living facility should be built, including the local waters, airs, temperatures, sun and shadow. In addition to the biblical flood, medieval writers attributed shortening of the lifespan to the atmosphere (Talmadge, 1990) or changes in the earth's density and gravitational field (Cohausen, 1771: 16).

From the time of the ancients, there has been a dispute over whether or not to place fate and body in the hands of medicine and physicians. Bacon's translator Browne wrote that "Old Age . . . is itself a disease." He proposed what many old people do today: go to doctors routinely to monitor their bodily states rather than going only when they have pain or distress (1653: A3). Maimonides, in the twelfth to thirteenth centuries, "advised older people to see a physician regularly" (Freeman, 1979: 27). But both Browne and Maimonides also recommended balance, moderation and a lack of excesses for old bodies.

Other experts warned old people away from physicians. James Easton wrote that "it is not the rich and great, but those who depend on medicine, who become old" (1799: xi). Easton recommended exercise as well as sobriety for old people, a change from earlier writers who believed that exercise used up the constant amount of vital heat that people were born with; women lived longer than men because they "stirred less." Cornaro, in several sixteenth-century self-help manuals on aging, temperance and moderation, recounts how he ate and drank, in his youth, to the point of obesity and inaction. He credited a moderate diet with no alcohol, long walks up and down hills, and horseback riding for his living into his eighties and beyond (1799): 2–45].

Male body-expertise continued into modern times, with ever-changing prescriptions. Eighteenth-century doctors cautioned women against moving around too much or too vigorously in case they damaged their reproductive organs. Victorian physicians warned against women riding bicycles, worrying that they would look unladylike and perhaps have illicit orgasms on the bicycle seat. Modern experts exhort us all to move around all the time, take vigorous exercise and treat sitting around as a form of cancer—and encourage women to have orgasms on bicycle seats or wherever they might wish.

Women's practical health has historically been, in Western culture, in the hands of women healers and midwives. But it was men who were the physicians and authors, with a few rare exceptions. Over the centuries there have been some women whose words joined those of men in the instruction of bodies. Merit Ptah, around 2700 BCE, was describe as the "Chief Physician" of Egypt. In Greece, Agnodike, in the fourth century BCE, was the first woman to practice legally as a physician; Metrodora, about six centuries later, wrote *On the Diseases and Cures of Women*. Hildegard of Bingen, of Germany, was as famous in the twelfth century for her medical writings as for her musical compositions.

With the coming of the Enlightenment, the position of women in society began to improve, with more access to education. And by the industrial revolution, women were knocking at the doors of medical schools and universities. Women's voices joined men's in the chorus of expertise and control over women's bodies and reproductive capabilities, culminating in the development and expansion of birth control. We grew up in the 1950s, '60s and '70s reading Simone de Beauvoir, Betty Friedan, Sylvia Plath, Germaine Greer and Gloria Steinem. These feminists grappled with issues of sexuality, reproduction, marriage and children in the context of the patriarchal family. When we were young, and these feminist authors were young, "body" was isomorphic with sexuality and reproduction in the context of romantic relationships. The vagina and the clitoris, orgasms, menstruation, contraception, abortion, giving birth, sexual exploration and identity—these bodily elements, in different combinations, were significant in young women's lives and writing. Youth, health and relative beauty were assumed.

Now that we are old, several items in this list have been crossed off: menstruation, contraception, giving birth. Clitoris and vagina are probably still present, but there may be no more ovaries or uterus. Orgasms, sexual exploration and identity, partners and spouses may still be around. But the sexual/relational body is only a (sometimes small) part of a host of bodily concerns. The whole body, and all its parts, become problematic in old age, both medically and cosmetically, reflected in the absence of old age in the mass and social media.

The mass media glorify youth and slenderness. The internet and social media share the culture's focus on youth but also contain a shadowland of divergences. Granny Porn is a click away from anyone on the internet (so, for that matter, is Grandpa Porn). Both the hetero-movie "Harold and Maude" and the homo-movie "Gerontophilia" depict people in their twenties sexually involved with the elderly, a "deviation" so rare that Kinsey does not mention it—although Krafft-Ebbing and John Money do briefly (Bering, 2013). We note this shadowland in passing, but we are not going to go there. We are interested in the mass and social media as they glorify the young body while ignoring or denigrating the old. We are not willing to spend a lot of time researching mass media depictions of gender, youth and age, but we do leaf through magazines when we are waiting at the beauty parlor. It is not easy to speak of the absence of something, but old women do seem absent from fashion advertising and magazines.

A March 2016 issue of the magazine *Elle* weighs in at 510 glossy 8- by 11-inch pages. The majority of the issue is advertising, with a few articles. Women who look no older than 25—and as young as 14—are on every page and in every advertisement, even the (many) for hair dye. They are short and tall, mostly white with some African-Americans and Asians, but they are all slender. The advertisements are mainly for clothing, jewelry, accessories such as handbags, makeup, skin creams and hair products. Some of the advertisements feature handsome young men along with beautiful young women; one has the young women paired with a silver-haired man. There is one small picture of a fat woman, a contributor to one of the articles. And there is a small picture of 69-year-old Sally Field, looking disheveled but youthful, as the star of a new movie.

The Spring 2016 glossy for old people, the *AARP Magazine*, also features Sally Field, on the cover and inside. She is slender and smiling with perfectly white and even teeth; her long hair is brown, streaked expertly with blond. She looks like a schoolgirl in her pleated skirt. Eighty-four-year-old Loretta Lynn, on page 56 of the magazine, has long dark hair, perfect teeth, smooth skin, red lips and a slender body; she is dressed in youthful jeans, boots and jacket. In this issue of the magazine there are a few photographs in articles and advertisements of men with white or gray hair, but only two advertisements featuring white-haired women. And this is the American Association for Retired People. As Pappas (2011) summarizes:

> If you're over 50 and pick up a copy of Vogue magazine, don't expect to see someone like you peering back from the cover . . . fashion magazines portray women over 40 sparingly, if at all.

Fifty—and how about 70 or 80, even in the *AARP Magazine*.

The object of the glossy media, whether fashion or housewifery, is to sell products for their advertisers. Although old people have considerable buying power and buy everything from night cream to expensive cruises, most of them are not glamorous enough to do the selling. Young or young-looking women with long, glorious hair sell hair dye, and women with flawless skin sell products designed to minimize flaws. We won't give examples, because we don't want to do product placement. And you can see it for yourself the next time you browse through the magazines at a salon. Susan Bordo, who is about 70, has claimed for the past several decades that young and old women are vulnerable to the public culture of the body. She refers to

> The endless commercials and advertisements that we believe we pay no attention to [while we are] [o]n the bus, in the airport, at the checkout line.
>
> (2003: 1)

The point is that although old women are not depicted in the mass media, young ones are—and they provide unattainable models for imperfect young and all old women.

Amanda Hess (2017) points out that the messages of marketing anti-aging products and procedures to old women have varied over time. In the 1920s and '30s, advertisements were cautionary tales: if a woman of 22 did not use Palmolive skin cream, she would be one of the "girls with empty date books"; if married, she would "lose love." Today the language is militarized: we, brave women, combat or fight wrinkles. What remains the same:

> We nod and agree that we should embrace our wrinkles, while quietly understanding that none of us individually . . . wants to be the one who actually looks old.

Television and the movies not only display anti-aging products, they display young faces and bodies as exemplars of how women should look. Brooks (2017) discusses soap operas, reality shows and celebrity culture as they affect her, and other women's, evaluation of their faces and bodies. She says:

> The rise of reality television is widely credited with toppling soap operas' supreme reign. But it also overwhelms us with cosmetically altered like never before.
>
> (p. 195)

Celebrity women, who want to keep their jobs as actors, are both consumers and role models of anti-aging procedures.

Some movies and television programs that star old women and enable them to continue working in entertainment; "Golden Girls" was a staple sitcom in the 1980s. Today, there is the British series "Last Tango in Halifax," which centers around two people nearing 80 who reconnect and remarry, and the ripple effect on and from their various adult offspring. "Grace and Frankie" stars Sam Waterston, Martin Sheen, Lily Tomlin and Jane Fonda. Tomlin and Fonda play 70-year-olds, although they are closer to 80. "Grace and Frankie," of these three sitcoms, focuses most directly on issues of body, adornment and cosmetic surgery. Lily Tomlin embodies the "Boho" approach to aging, resembling an old hippie draped in layers of clothing, with long, graying hair. Jane Fonda exemplifies the fight against aging, with her never-eating slender body, sculpted face and carefully coiffed blond hair. They are exemplars of the search for youth, and targets of feminist critiques of the way women age.

There is a culture war among feminists between those who insist that old (and for that matter young) women should not adopt any of Western culture's body norms, and those who allow that minimal body modification is OK. This culture war is somewhat divided between young feminists, who have no need of face-lifts and tummy tucks, and old feminists, some of whom (but not Germaine Greer) allow the possibility of some intervention, whether the low bar be face cream or hair dye. Spar (2016), who at 53 is the president of Barnard College, admits to having had some cosmetic surgery. She says:

> These days, at least in Manhattan . . . many women will quietly confess to a shot of Botox from time to time, or a dose of filler to soften their smiles. It's after that point that things become dodgy. Brow lifts. Estrogen. Tummy tucks . . . cellulite treatment. Is it all a kind of slippery slope to some kind of Kardashian hell? . . . Does a little face-lift along the way constitute treason, or just a reasonable accommodation? I don't know.

Although old people are rare in magazine advertising and articles, they can be heard or seen on various internet websites. There are local, state and national "Senior Ms." beauty pageants for women 60 and over. They pose in photographs and in person wearing ball gowns and high heels, although not swimsuits. Many of them are slender, blond or dark haired as they pose for the judges; others have white hair and larger bodies. The judging categories are appearance, talent and the wisdom of old age in what some of the pageant organizers call "the age of elegance."

There are also numerous .com sites where issues of aging are raised and comments made, including body and sexual concerns. An article in the British tabloid *The Daily Mail* about the sex lives (or lack of them) of four old women featured pictures of the women in glamorous dresses, with long dark hair, red lips and fingernails, nylon stockings and high heeled shoes. Jeannette, 72, says that "The reality of the sexual landscape in later life" is this:

> [economic] 'equals' of the same age mainly had their sights set on some 25 year old . . . . Most of the men who have come knocking at my door . . . seem to be silently evaluating my house or looking for a nursemaid.

Comments on this article varied. Most were positive, such as one man who said "Good for them," and several who wanted the phone numbers of the single women. There were many comments on how wonderful— as in not-old—the women looked, although with caveats; one man said that "These ladies look gorgeous—with their clothes ON!" But other men's comments were not so positive:

> "Yuck! Who in their right mind would want to read about old women and their love lives."

> "Old people should not be having sex."

> "Disgusting, leave sex to the young please, you've had your day."

> "Do these women have no shame."

These youthfully-adorned women "looked good" to some of the bloggers—albeit with their clothes on. But internet trolls search and find fault with any fat or old women appearing in the mass or social media.

Mary Beard, a 60-ish Cambridge classics professor, appeared on television in the United Kingdom looking like the "don" that she is, with long gray hair; one social media troll called her "ugly." She was also a guest on a radio program called "Going Grey" (Schneier, 2016: 9). Oliver Rawlings, a 21-year-old internet troll, tweeted that she was "a filthy old slut." Dr. Beard responded that one of the "rights of women" is "to look, even in her fifties, like her unvarnished self . . . you are looking at a 59 year old woman. That is what 59 year old women who have not had work done look like. Get it?" (p. 8). Mary Beard and Oliver Rawlings had a happy ending. Mary forgave Oliver after he apologized in person, even writing him a letter of recommendation for a job (Hermann, 1014). Schneier (2016), who interviewed Mary Beard, seems anxious to portray her as other than a frump, describing her as "silver" rather than gray haired. He describes her as "hardly the 'old frump' of an earlier era of British academia" in her red shoes and (Danish designer Bitte Kai Rand) canary yellow coat. As we will see throughout this book, attention to adornment is one way in which old women attempt to deflect attention from their aging bodies

Carrie Fisher first played Princess Leia in "Star Wars" when she was 19. At 59, she reprised the part, along with 73-year-old Harrison Ford. Twitter trolls made comments such as "You didn't age well" and "U Sucked in Star Wars" (Telegraph Films, 2015). Among her Twitter responses: "my BODY has not aged as well as I have," and "Youth&BeautyR/NOT ACCOMPLISHMENTS." Ms. Fisher says that she had to lose weight to be cast in *The Force Awakens*: "They didn't want to hire all of me—only about three quarters!" There were no similar tweets about Harrison Ford; old men are not immune to the ravages of age or the pitter-patter of trolls, but old women make much better targets.

If you have an old woman's face and body, you are damned if you do and damned if you don't. Mary Beard was trolled for not coloring her hair or undergoing a face-lift, and Carrie Fisher for looking plump and middle aged. But if old women do have their faces lifted and their hair colored, they are equally the subject of criticism. At the 2014 Oscars, trolls engaged in body and face shaming of several old women. Donald Trump tweeted that 81-year-old Kim Novak should sue her plastic surgeon ("Kim Novak Takes on Oscar Night Bullies," 2014). Liza Minelli—"nipped, lifted and filled" at 67—was mocked as a drag queen by Ellen DeGeneres, who noted that "the most important thing in the world is youth." Matthew McConaughey's mother was taunted for her cleavage, which was described as "leathery" and "terrifying" (Hess, 2014).

There are mass and social media niches where old age is neither invisible nor denigrated but glorified or at least admired. TV programs and movies starring admirable old women or men are not hard to find; if we were to do an inventory it would fill volumes. But we think that if such an inventory were done, it would feature dyed perhaps more than white or gray hair, wrinkles arguably less than filler-smoothed skin—Jane Fonda as well as Lily Tomlin. Celebrating wrinkles and gray or white hair is unusual, but not unknown. Pinterest has a board for "1000+ . . . Beautiful Old People," with 202 pinned images and 783 followers. There are portrait photographs of extremely wrinkled old women and men, together with a saying from Mark Twain: "Wrinkles should merely indicate where smiles should be." Perhaps this quote is an attempt to combat ageism; if so, it does not work for us.

The internet can be a source of information for as well as denigration or admiration of old women. Women—old and young—can and do find answers to their bodily questions on the internet. There are sites such as https://embarrassingquestions.com where a user can type in a question and get an answer and perhaps some further sources of information. And there are blogs where multiple people post questions, answers and comments. One English thread, for example, is called "Old Feminists Speak: Experiences of Aging." The site is https://ageingageismdiary.wordpress.com. An anonymous old woman says:

> God knows why I took the online test, 'What Is Your Real Age'? Do I need to have a test to know my own age? I was born . . . 81 years . . . ago. The test gave me a bloody age of 85. . . . the blooming cheek!

This British 81-year-old demonstrates, and Mary Beard concludes, that a little humor goes a long way towards handling both the outrages of aging, and the outrages of the trolls and the do-gooders. "American feminism needs more wry humor. . . . The outrage meter is getting out of control "(Schneier, 2016: 9).

In addition to the media, there are proximate, embodied examples of youthful aging among the old women. We are talking with Iris, a slender, well-dressed, bejeweled woman of 73, whose hair is colored blonde and whose eyes are carefully outlined and mascara-ed. Caroline walks in and sits at a barstool a few seats away. She is slender and of medium height, with soft brown hair that must be but does not look dyed. She is very beautiful, with a shining white-toothed smile and bright, expressive green eyes. Iris says, "she looks so great for her age."

Carol: "How old is she?" (thinking perhaps 60).
Iris: "She is seventy-three, my age, and she looks better than me!"

Old women who want to embody the ideal of a young, slender body and lovely face can leaf through magazines, troll the internet or perch on barstools to see the competition. The other side of the competition is old women who look less slender, youthful and lovely than Iris, or Caroline or any of the old women. Although these women are rarely present in magazines, they can be found in the internet and on your local barstool.

Old women may be invisible (in the mass media), admired (on Pinterest and Granny Porn, or on a barstool), denigrated (by ancient and modern men, or by their peers) or scolded for their attempts to seem youthful and for their competitiveness in this endeavor. But we are getting old regardless of what we do or do not do. Our naked bodies are observed in the mirror or in bed, and our adorned bodies are observed and commented on wherever we go. In the chapters that follow, we take note of the old body's structures and functions, height and weight, public display, private moments and sensations of pain and pleasure. We look the old women in the eye, and we look at their eyes. We speak and hear, touch and embrace—and, above all, we are with one another.

PART I
THE PRIVATE BODY

2
THE EDIFICE
From Skeleton to Skin

Our body is our self. Our body is an edifice, our skeleton clothed by muscles, flesh and skin, propelled into motion with every breath we take. The edifice moves—we walk, arms swing, we sit; and the edifice functions. Inside the body there are organs and systems that we know exist but do not see, such as our nervous system with its neural network and our circulatory system with heart and blood vessels. And there are systems which we feed and feel, notably the digestive and urinary, as well as the sexual, once-reproductive system—the terrain of *Our Bodies Ourselves*. We begin with this sexual terrain, because it is central to ourselves as women. Then we return to those parts of the body common to all humans (yet with special gendered twists and turns): the skeleton and the flesh built upon it, the skin and digestive and urinary systems, and the breath that animates motion.

Our bodies and genitals may be in sexual as well as social relationships. In *Our Bodies Ourselves*, the authors discussed topics ranging from marriage and household chores to bisexuality and child rearing. In this chapter, we explore the bodily aspects of the sexual (that is no longer reproductive), from pubic hair to genitalia and orgasm. In Chapter 6, we take up the theme of these old women's bodies as they appear in the mirror of sexual relationships, as well as the mirror of non-sexual social relationships. The places where our naked bodies are observed, touched and pleasured, and our clothed bodies are judged and compared—we are observed from skeleton to skin.

Young women have a reproductive apparatus consisting of uterus, cervix, ovaries, vagina, labia and clitoris, protected by a mons pubis and pubic hair. Old women no longer menstruate, and they generally cannot bear children without extraordinary medical intervention. Thus, sanitary pads, tampons and contraceptives are not needed. One of the joys of passing through menopause to the other side is the lack of monthly bleeding and all the arrangements and purchases and discomforts that surround menstruation. Annette, 72, says: "When I was young I bled horribly for about two weeks every month. I had to wear tampons and pads and change them constantly. By the time I was sixty I was free of all that. It was and is wonderful." Sheila Nevins (2017: 181), at 56, writes of the cessation of menstruation. Her poem about "Eunice" celebrates no longer worrying about getting pregnant or about the possibility of menstrual blood staining her white clothing.

When we first see a naked female body from the front, we see, first, the pubic hair or lack of it. The old woman's external genitalia may be no different than when she was young, but her mons pubis is likely to be gray, thinning, or bald. And it was a conversation about body hair that provided the spark for this book.

> We are sitting and standing around the bar talking: Kathi and Carol, Wilma, 70, and Eve, Kathleen and Caroline, all in their eighties. Wilma's, Eve's and Caroline's husbands were also there, talking about the sports event showing on the TV. The women's conversation started with an upcoming cruise to the Bahamas. Eve said that she no longer had to shave her underarms because she had no more hair there. Caroline chimed in: "I used to have to shave my underarms and legs and now I don't. I used to have hairy arms, but I don't have those any longer." Eve: "I have one hair under one arm that I have to shave." Wilma laughed nervously as the conversation paused before the next frontier—but nobody went there. Caroline: "I have three long hairs on one leg." Kathleen: "They never told us any of this, did they?" A chorus of, "No, they did not."

"They," whoever they are, did not tell us body hair would disappear or that the pubic hair of old women would thin and/or go gray and white with the passing of the decades, nor were we, when young, in a position to observe the process.

The generations of Western culture have given us different instructions about our pubes. Like their Egyptian predecessors, Greek women plucked their pubic hairs out as soon as they appeared; a hairy mons was considered unfeminine. Roman women—at least the courtesans—followed the same practice. But with the fall of the Empire came the return of pubic hair as a symbol of sexuality. In the fifteenth century, prostitutes shaved off their pubic hair because of lice, but wore merkins, or pubic wigs Waxman, 2011). Women's pubic hair fell in and out of favor in public life and in the arts from the sixteenth to the twentieth centuries. In the 1970s, *Penthouse* magazine was publishing pictures of women's pubic hair, but by the 1980s pornography began to portray the hairless mons. According to informants who know about this kind of thing, pornography featuring female pubic hair is listed under "perversions."

As Friedland (2011) points out, women who are now around 70 came of age when the lushness of pubic hair was one of the sexual attributes of young and burgeoning—albeit dangerous—sexuality. Pubic hair represented what we guarded and what boys wanted. But among the younger generations—teens through forties—a majority now appear to favor a waxed or shaved mons. By the 2000s, there were sexually active young men who had never encountered women with pubic hair. Complete pubic baldness, once the symbol of childhood, has now been extended to youth and adult sexuality as well as to the very old. But in-between childhood and advanced age is a stage signaling the onset of old age: our thinning and graying public hair. Poet Sharon Olds has written several odes about the old body (2016), including the "Merkin Ode" (p. 84) about her aging mons—her "shrub"—which she imagines as weeds being whacked by time.

We observe the changes in our shrub. When pubic hair is mentioned around the old women, they raise their eyebrows or roll their eyes. Ruby: "What pubic hair?" Some of them accept the state of their shrub, while others get rid of it by waxing or shaving—thus mimicking the contemporary youthful body. Viola, who is nearing 60 and has a boyfriend in his thirties, shaves her pubic hair in order to eliminate the thinning and graying evidence of the advance of age. Eve waxes her pubic hair so as not to showcase gray wisps, thus imitating, simultaneously, childhood, contemporary young womanhood and advanced old age. Wilma, 70, says, "I do that too. My husband shaves my pubic hair . . . he has been doing it since we were first married." One 70-year-old woman says that her pubic hair is still lush, but it is gray, which she does not like.

The mons pubis, with or without hair, protects or showcases a woman's labia minora and majora and clitoris. As women age, the labia may become dryer than in youth, or even painful. There are many medical conditions that can cause itching and sore legions on the labia, including genital herpes and several skin diseases. But older women may suffer from "vulval pain syndrome," or "vulvodynia"—the soreness and itching are unremitting, but "no one knows what causes it" Annette's doctor told her: "we have checked you for everything and you don't have anything. We can give you some creams to try."

"Wattles"—fleshy lobes of tissue that resemble poultry parts—often appear on aging faces, necks, and limbs. They may also appear on an aging genital-urinary system. Old women's urethras may play host to caruncles—aka wattles—fleshy excrescences that may cause problems from bleeding to pain. Carol found it interesting that a urinary specialist knew about caruncles, but her GP did not—and neither did her gynecologist or gynecological nurse practitioner. And a GP or gynecologist who does not know about caruncles can become very concerned about bleeding in old women and order all kinds of tests. Carol was tested for urinary cancer during a two-month period before the caruncle was diagnosed.

And then there is the place of the private parts in sexual activity, sore, wattled or balding. The vaginal lubrication characteristic of youthful sexual arousal may diminish after menopause. Some old women do not experience vaginal dryness. Other postmenopausal women do. Sarah Crichton, seeking a new sexual relationship in her early sixties, says that "If my goal is to return to an easy state of play I need to consider hormone replacement therapy" (2016: 96). Tessa, 71, says that she remains on HRT for "vaginal receptivity." Both these women are willing to risk the medical complications of HRT for the sake of their male partners' sexual pleasure.

For many of the old women, only the vagina was mentioned in what passed for sex education prior to *Our Bodies Ourselves*; the role of the clitoris in sexual stimulation and orgasm was not taught. Some women found this out all by themselves, but other young women in 1970 needed *Our Bodies Ourselves* to understand the physiology of female sexual response. The "plug-in-socket" theory and practice of sexual congress left them without orgasm, and they were unaware of the importance of the clitoris to sexual satisfaction—unlike men, who can readily observe their penises, erections, and ejaculations. Annette says, "I learned to masturbate when I was twenty-six. I had not had any orgasm before that because I had not clarified what or where my clitoris was. I discovered it when a friend told me about her vibrator." By 70, women may—or may not—be aware of what or where their clitoris is, and they may—or may not—seek and achieve orgasms, in or outside of relationships.

Women's orgasms and sexual response have been the contested terrain of male experts throughout recorded history. Clitoridectomies throughout cultures and ages have ensured that women be denied sexual pleasure and thus not be tempted to "stray" from their husbands. They were performed in Europe and the United States until the early twentieth century and remain in practice in certain African and Middle Eastern countries to the present day. In psychoanalysis, although the clitoris was not removed from the body, its sexual significance was banished. Freud theorized that there were two types of orgasm: clitoral and the more "mature" vaginal. Although this theory has been discredited, early disciples of Freud believed it. Applying theory to practice, one disciple, Marie Bonaparte, resorted to surgery to move her clitoris closer to her vaginal opening (this seems like cheating to us).

In the 2000s, the medicalizing male gaze has lighted upon the labia and its structural imperfections, which in turn require surgical intervention. In labiaplasty, the labia majora and/or minora are "surgically cut and altered in the name of symmetry and beautification. By 2014, these surgeries had almost doubled since the previous year (Brooks, 2017: 208). Brooks suggests that the trend toward the hairless mons pubis has increased the popularity of these surgeries; now that the genitals are no longer hidden by hair, "their 'imperfections' are fully exposed and fair game for cosmetic intervention" (Brooks, 2017: 209). Unlike clitoridectomies, labiaplasties are chosen by the women who have them rather than by other men or women. None of the women we know have mentioned having this kind of surgery, although one 74-year-old woman discusses hers on a YouTube video.

The marketplace, too, has seized upon the female genitalia. Gunter (2017: 57) discusses women's discomfort with their—as she, as a gynecologist, says—perfectly normal vaginas. Women can shop for vaginal (and anal) bleaches, tightening sticks (which dry out the vagina), steaming, glitter and douches (an older product). Women are advised to be concerned about the looseness, wetness and smell of their private parts. In the 1950s, women were advised to return to being "the girl he married" by using Lysol. Today's version of an anti-odor product is Vicks VapoRub. Gunter says of young women:

> I know you stand in drugstores wondering why there are all these hygiene products if they are unnecessary. I know you stare into the internet, and wonder, if celebrities say they steam their vaginas, or have 10-step vaginal prep regimens, then maybe vaginal neglect really is a flaw that ruins relationships.

We can only hope that the old women do not join them.

Women between the end of menopause and the age of 100 do not have to worry about menstruation or pregnancy. But they may be sexually active and desire sexual pleasure and orgasm. Lily, 71, noted that she still had vaginal spasms during orgasm. Ruby said, after her total hysterectomy at 74, "it did not seem to affect anything" about orgasm once sexual activity could be resumed. What may change over time, with aging, is the ability to reach orgasm easily. Intercourse may not work even if it once did; manual, oral or vibrator stimulation may be more effective.

Little is known of the orgasmic functioning of old women, perhaps seen as less important than their digestive or urinary systems. Anyone can look at Granny Porn, at their naked partner or at themselves in the mirror, but otherwise the bodies and sexual practices of the old women are veiled from public view. Betty Friedan (1993) discusses a study done by one of her gerontology students, in which six women over 65 without partners were asked about several sexual and orgasmic options including "self-sex or masturbation" (p. 268). These women were not amused. One woman said that "God would punish" old women who sought an orgasm through self-stimulation. Our old women did not, generally, talk about masturbation, but some wrote about it. Anne, 74, divorced twice and widowed once, with no current partner, says in response to a question about orgasm, "masturbation works for me when I am feeling good."

Studies and surveys often use ambiguous language, so that any "findings" will also be ambiguous. Lily is part of a large-scale longitudinal study of "healthy aging," which includes questions about "sex" as well as other relationship topics. One question is "How satisfied are you with your sex life?" with numbered levels of satisfaction. Lily does not answer this question on the surveys because she is not sure what it refers to:

> I wonder what they mean by "sex life"? Do they mean orgasms? Intercourse? Something else? I don't know what they mean by "satisfied." As opposed to angry, or as opposed to over the moon, or? And how do I assign a number to my "level" of satisfaction?' Do they mean satisfied that day, or do they mean for the past month?

We know not what they mean.

As we saw in Chapter 1, the old woman's desire for a sexual relationship is likely to be hampered by the lack of available partners. As Betty Friedan (1993: 254) said of her old age, "I felt the pain of my own yearning" for intimacy and sex. Among the old women we know who are alone and want to "date," many find nobody to date. Couples may find themselves in the opposite situation: together, but suspected of having no sexual lives. We are familiar with this trope when it comes to old people and their adult offspring, but it may also occur among peers.

> We are chatting at one table, and a married couple we know are at another table. Eve looks over at them and says: "I wonder if they do it? I always wonder if people our age do it."

One woman in her eighties says of her recent marriage, that sexually "we have a lot of fun. Nobody knows that."

Women's bodies, like men's, grow and age from skeleton to skin. Although men and women have skeletons and skin, digestive and urinary systems, and lungs that keep us breathing, there are gender differences in bodily aging beyond the genital. Skin, for example, ages for men and for women, with wrinkles appearing on the face and body. And that skin grows, or refuses to grow, hair. Men and women become bald; women grow hair on their chin and upper lip. All is turned upside down, as the old women see it. From skeleton to skin, we take a look at the aging woman's body.

We have all seen pictures of human skeletons—or we have seen actual ones—so we know what the edifice looks like. We know that the body is supposed to stand upright—but, as we age, some of us can no longer do so. The "stooped" skeleton of the old man or woman, as mocked by Erasmus, can result from bone conditions, bad posture or both. We notice how many daily activities, typically done by women throughout life, contribute to eyes and head angled downward: sweeping floors, setting tables, reaching for toddlers. We remind ourselves and each other to stand up straight. LouAnn, 81, asked Carol what medical condition was responsible for her stooped posture. She replied "Nothing. It's habit—spending years in the Kansas wind with my head down." Carol tells herself twenty times a day to stand up straight; but by now it feels unnatural: knees push back; back pushes forward; neck pushes back; shoulders go back, breasts go forward. But the stoop returns. Whenever Alice sees Carol stooping, she says, "Stand up straight." By 70, Alice had started to stoop; after her husband died, she said, laughing, "On that man's deathbed he told me to stand up straight."

Our stooped skeleton has many parts. It is well known that as we women age, our bones may become less dense and more liable to crack or break—medically known as "osteoporosis"—and there are quite a few prescription and non-prescription remedies for it. Tests for osteoporosis are recommended for women as they age. Kathi had one at 68 and was delighted with the result: "My doctor says I have the bones of a thirty-year-old." Osteoporosis coupled with bad posture and fat deposits can result in "dowager's hump," a curving of the back just below the neck. The condition is more common in women than men; for men, it is a "buffalo hump."

Our skeleton is propelled by joints, muscles, nerves and other aspects of the edifice; as children and young adults, we ran, jumped and played sports. As we age, motion may become more difficult. Stiff joints give us no end of trouble—the saying "I am feeling out of joint" reflects the grumpiness that can accompany the pain of arthritis and other conditions. Kathi's mother Peggy began to suffer from arthritis in her hands when she was in her fifties, referring to her "visits from Arthur." Our knees, hips, ankles and feet get a lot of wear over the years and are liable to multiple afflictions. Ruby and Nora, who are both 80, walk stiffly. Nora says, "I am healthy in every way except for arthritis. I have it in my hips. It hurts especially when I try to sleep." Eve walks fluidly, with perfect posture, but she grimaces when she gets up from a chair. Annette says: "It is difficult to get out of bed in the morning. I am so stiff that my back does not want to move, and my legs don't want to move either." Pain can lead to lack of sleep and immobility. Annette adds: "All the commotion at night, plus the horrible dreams— when I get out of bed in the morning I am exhausted!" (laughter).

Impaired motion is particularly problematic for women who have spent their lives in motion. Many women took care of their families, enjoying cooking for them and doing the housework. Hands crippled by time can no longer peel potatoes very well, adding to the old woman's sense of disassociation from her "real self" and place in the world (Williams and Warren, 2008). Some women were athletic when young, playing tennis or volleyball competitively or just for fun. Stiffness and pain in their knees and shoulders prevent them from enjoying the pleasures of the past. Kathi can still play tennis without difficulty; Carol worries about her knees if she plays and worries about what she has become when she does not play. Brenda, 85, and her husband George are both thin and of medium height. They walk a lot, and George rides a bicycle daily. They have a large powerboat docked behind their house, which they take along the coast every year. But this year was different:

George: "We are not going this year. Brenda's balance is not very good. She can get on and off the boat, but she can't get into or out of the dinghy without worrying about falling into the water or off the dock."

Sustaining motion is important to old people, and so is balance. Moving around on uneven surfaces such as bobbing boats or cobblestones can throw the old off balance unless they use a cane—which may be of use on cobblestones but not so much in the bobbing boat.

Elbows and knees enable the body to reach and to move. Since people do not walk on their hands, it is not surprising that elbows are less liable to severe problems than knees. But they are not free of issues. Elbows are sometimes afflicted by arthritis or by dislocation, and by sports. "Tennis elbow" is self-explanatory; "golf elbow" is less common but equally disturbing to the athletically inclined. Knees are one of the bellwethers of aging in motion, and they can be afflicted by dozens of conditions, from torn meniscus to pseudogout. Many, many of the old women have had knee replacements; sometimes two or three times per knee. Those who have, and those who have not, may hobble around on walkers, crutches and sticks for weeks or months at a time. Sharon Olds, a Pulitzer Prize-winning poet born in 1942, writes in her "Knee Replacement Ode" that although she is glad that she had the surgery, she wants to piece her old knee together again (p. 21). Her ode speaks of the yearning to be young and whole in body again.

Hips are another bellwether of aging in motion. Many of the old women have had hip replacements, in one or both hips, and many more will have them in the future. Nicole, 72, pulls down her jeans and panties to reveal a long scar towards her back: "that is what they had to do. I am doing OK, but it takes a while." Later, Nicole had to return to the hospital for a reparative surgery on that same hip, a not uncommon situation for the old women for both their knee and hip surgery. Annette says: "I am trying to deny that I am having hip pain. It is in the front of my hips rather than in the back like Nicole's." Rosie, 75, had successful knee surgery, but several weeks later she writes, "The pain seems to have migrated to the other side!! Both my hip and my knee!" About eight months later, though, she told us that she was free of pain and able to walk.

Working outward from the skeleton and joints toward the skin, we encounter the muscles. Our muscles fall victim over time to gravity, softening and drooping, even among slender women. The body turns to flab in parts before the whole—upper arms, then lower arms, then thighs, then calves. We are sitting at the bar chatting with Rae, 70, who is wearing a colorful long-sleeved jacket. We warn her that the talk she is waiting to hear is filling up, and perhaps "you should put your jacket on one of the chairs to save your space." "Oh no," she says, "I am not going to show my arms. I used to have beautiful arms, playing tennis all the time, very muscular, but not anymore." The incidence of surgical "arm lifts" rose almost 5,000% between 2000 and 2016 (www.plastic-surgery.org), although we don't know if any of the old women we know have had one.

By the mid-eighties, the entire body may lose significant muscle mass. Lee, 87, says that "I am not overweight. Unfortunately, I am a mass of flab." Flab, together with wrinkles, persuade many old women to cover their arms and legs at all times. Others are fully covered in public social situations but uncover for exercise:

As we are driving we notice a woman jogging on the sidewalk. She is short and thin, wearing a baseball hat with a blond ponytail pulled through, a tank top and short shorts. From a distance she looks like a young woman. As we get closer, we see that she is a woman we know, whom we had thought to be around 60. We also see that her well-shaped legs are a mass of grooved wrinkles. Perhaps she is 80. Perhaps she was once obese and lost a considerable amount of weight.

The only old people who appear able to halt the softening of the muscles without surgical interventions are professional bodybuilders: Charles Atlas and Jack LaLanne are the male prototypes. There are several female bodybuilders in their 70s whose arms, legs and torsos are strong and muscular. The oldest discussed by the media is Ernestine Shephard, who was still winning bodybuilding competitions at the age of 80 and can be found on YouTube and in the Guinness Book of Records. If the old woman wants to run 80 miles a week, work out for six hours a day and subsist on a diet of egg whites and nuts, she can escape some of the bodily ravages of time.

Many of the old women diet to remain slender; others go to the gym or walk a lot. A few still engage in challenging physical activities. Belinda, 70, is small and very thin, with carefully colored and coiffed blond hair piled atop her head in a chignon. Her abdomen is flat and she carries herself with grace and balance. She takes ballet lessons every weekday, using toe shoes part of the time. Kitty, who does other kinds of dance, admires Belinda: "Do you know how much strength it takes to dance in toe shoes?" Calasanti and King (2015: 196) point out that there is, in today's culture, almost a moral imperative for old people to exhibit "personal control" over the "beauty, and health" of their bodies through "technologies, diet and exercise, and consumer lifestyles." One 49-year-old woman comments that she doesn't "get why women would want to walk around in sweatpants with grey hair and no makeup" (Brooks, 2017: 51).

Beyond the muscles, the edifice's outer boundary—the skin—ages relentlessly, waiting for the remedies of diet, technologies and the marketplace. The aging of the skin starts with the face and hands, culminating in upper arm, upper leg, and finally lower arm, lower leg and even knee wrinkles. Aging is one cause of wrinkles as our natural oils dry out and the subcutaneous fat layers lessen; other causes include heredity, exposure to sun and weight. There is a saying among the old women: it is either your face or your butt. If you are fat (with a large butt) your face will be smooth; if you are thin (with a smaller butt) your face will be wrinkled. Smoking—past or present—involves a repeated sucking motion, which wears permanent grooves above the upper lip. As we will see in subsequent chapters, wrinkles on the face prompt many old women to seek skin treatments—as do age spots on face and hands—from creams to cosmetic surgery. We will encounter our wrinkled skin again when we discuss the public body.

Many yards of skin cover the edifice, and any part of it can torment or worry the old woman. There are medical conditions such as eczema and psoriasis that affect people of all ages; then there is "senile pruritis," the itching of the skin of the old, with no known cause. We scratch the itches, only to cause lesions which then scab over, causing more itching—the itch-scratch cycle of old skin. And then there are the skin eruptions that may or may not send us to the dermatologist:

Carol: "I have things come up all over my arms in addition to the age spots. They are blue, green brown. When I pointed them out to my doctor; she would look at them and give them a name that sounded like a character in a Russian novel. The spots usually would disappear. Now I don't bother anymore."

Skin also gets more allergic over time:

Carol: "Nice earrings. Are they real?"
Natasha (30): "I can only wear real gold, my ears get allergic to metal."
Carol: "I was first allergic to base metal, then to sterling silver, and then to gold. Now I can't wear any earrings."
Natasha groans. Carol refrains from adding that her neck is now becoming allergic, making the wearing of necklaces difficult.

"Thin skin" is a metaphor—its origins in the seventeenth century—for emotional oversensitivity or touchiness. But it is also a physical condition of the old. There are parts of the body, such as the abdomen, whose fat layers (and positioning) protect against skin damage; other parts, such as the shins and elbows, become more and more fragile. As old people trip, fall, and knock against things they risk various kinds of damage, including skin lesions and bleeding. Carol has fallen on her knees so many times that there is not much left between skin and knee bone. Eve skinned her shin while folding her tall body into the back of an SUV, shaving two inches of skin and causing profuse bleeding. While some skin wounds heal, there is always the risk of infection for the old women. Another affliction of thin old skin is bruising. Rosie's forearms are always covered in purple bruises. She says, "it is not too bad at the moment, unless I start having to take medications." Old people bump their arms and legs into things, causing capillary breakage and consequent bruising.

Between the skin, the joints, the muscles and the skeleton are the functioning systems: heart and lungs, blood passageways, kidneys and liver. We consider in this chapter only those functioning systems that have a social and observable aspect: the digestive (eating, throwing up, flatulence, defecating), the urinary (drinking and peeing), the sexual and the breath that allows the body to live. All these systems functioned unnoticed, most of the time, when we were young, bothersome only so far as they needed daily and routine ingestion, excretion and cleaning. Maybe we drank alcohol and took drugs, but we did so with relative impunity; not so the elderly drinker or drug user, who suffers many more complications. *Our Bodies Ourselves* was written to help young women understand their bodies in cultural context, focusing on the sexual, reproductive and relational. For the old women, sexual and social relationships may (or may not) be important, but their digestive and urinary systems demand at least equal attention.

The ingestions and excretions of our old digestive systems, beginning with eating and ending with defecation—and sometimes thence to incontinence. It is not enough, today, to be moderate in our eating and drinking habits. We women live in a world of "health advice," highlighted by media and marketing. Within the past few years there has been a vast expansion of the concept of "gluten-free" eating, shored up by the production of a mass of gluten-free products from bread to pasta—and then there are paleo, vegan and raw food options. Old people with digestive symptoms are prime targets for the latest food fads marketed on television, in magazines and on the internet. As we will see in the next chapter, we are also ripe, if we are fat, for the latest diet fads.

We know some young vegans and a few old vegetarians, but it is gluten free that attracts the old women, at least in the mid-twenty-first century. The March 2016 issue of the glitzy *Allure* magazine went so far as to advertise, on p. 79, gluten-free shampoo. But it is food intake that is generally the issue. At a party:

> Alice is pointing out foods: "These are gluten free" pointing at some crackers, "and so are these," referring to corn chips." "Oh I want to do that," says one of the women, "what does it do?" "I was always bloated and now I am not," Alice replied.

However, Alice's bloating did not disappear, and she had intestinal surgery, in the course of which pre-cancerous polyps were removed.

The dangers inherent in self-diagnosis are clear in this and other stories. Marnie, 56, was suffering for months with bloating and was advised by friends to avoid gluten, which she did for several more months. Her problem persisted, however, so she went to a doctor, who gave her various diagnoses and treatment. After six months of being told she had various abdominal problems, Marnie was diagnosed with Stage 4 ovarian cancer.

A woman's food intake is contested by "experts" throughout her lifespan. "Eating disorders" such as bulimia or anorexia (Bordo, 2003) are the bookend of youth; tube- or force-feeding the bookend of old age—although, as we will see in the next chapter, anorexia has been identified in the old. People are plied with experts' nutritional advice and advertising throughout the life course, with specialized niches for gender and age, from supplements to protein drinks that can take the place of food. Old people may have problems with the taste and smell of food or a dementia-driven inability to remember if one has eaten or not. In residential facilities for the aged, staff are there to ensure that old people eat; this may not be the case for couples and individuals who live in their homes—even if they have high incomes. Norma, 90, says, "We have a girl who comes in and cooks, but she is a terrible cook, so we end up throwing most of what she cooks away."

Once inside the body, food can cause a variety of problems for aging digestive systems, including food sensitivity or allergies, constipation or diarrhea, and burping or flatulence. These problems of bodily functioning can occur at any age but may cause more havoc among the old. There are innumerable food-borne illnesses that can affect people of any age, but they often strike the very old, as well as the very young, more severely than young and middle-aged people. Although allergies and food sensitivities are associated with children and young people, these may appear at any age, including old age. Carol, at age 73, had a somewhat unexpected anaphylactic shock reaction to eating a shrimp; she stopped breathing until her body rejected the guilty shrimp.

What was pleasurable to eat when young, and still desired, may be problematic for the old body. Eve says, "I have always loved chocolate. I still love chocolate. I still eat chocolate. But if I do, now it gives me acid indigestion." Many old women say that they have become lactose intolerant as they age and are now unable to drink milk or eat yogurt, ice cream or cheese at all, or without the help of (well-marketed) capsules of various kinds. Again, self-diagnosis is the norm. Clarissa, 75, says: "I can't eat cheese anymore because I have eaten so much of it all my life that I have become lactose intolerant." Carol: "Is that a diagnosis, and did you get tested?" Clarissa: "No, it is MY diagnosis."

Old men and women often have more problems with belching and with flatulence than they did during adulthood, with public "slips"—hence the sayings "burpy old person" and "Old Fart." Burping may be caused by rapid eating and carbonated beverages; it may seem "natural" (especially among boys, who gulp their food and drink) until it becomes "excessive" in old age (moderation in all things). Those same young boys who burp after every ingestion may also delight in farting as often and loudly as possible. But the old people would prefer not to—and yet we do.

Old people's digestive systems are slower than when we were young, which causes more gas—especially if we eat a lot of those foods deemed best for our nutrition, such as pulse foods, vegetables, fruits and whole grains (Bennet, 2012). This is only one of the ironies of food and age: what we are supposed to consume to remain healthy may be exactly what will cause us to have digestive problems such as burping and farting. Old women comment on the flatulence of old age:

Johna: "I find that occasionally I'll let out a fart without thinking."

> Public farting is one of those characteristics of old age that makes young people think we are icky and socially hopeless. Of course, it will happen to them, as well, but we'll all be long dead by then.
> (Bennet, 2012)

Public farting is a humiliating bodily event for people other than young boys, so that the old women talk about it only rarely. Annette: "I let out farts fairly frequently when I walk around. If there are people nearby, I just hope they don't hear me." Discussing the problems of having roommates on cruises or in hotel rooms, 75-year-old Clarissa says, "I tell them they won't want to spend their nights listening to snoring and farting."

Constipation can afflict people of any age, but the problem may increase with aging. Peristalsis is slowed down by the progression of years and also may be affected by various medications that old people take. Rosie always has prunes on the table for breakfast at home; Lily has a laxative to combat the effects of the statins she takes. We are advised to eat more fiber and drink more water—but as we age, eating more fiber can cause diarrhea, and drinking more water keeps us up at night. The husband of a woman in her eighties says: "She does not eat salads any more, she always used to eat salads. They give her diarrhea." It was probably good for this man's health that the woman in question was away from the dining table at the time.

We eat, and we drink. The urinary system involves the ingestion, processing and excretion of liquids, from milk to coffee to wine to vodka—and perhaps to leakage and incontinence. Liquids of various types can cause problems for the body at any age, but age may exacerbate or multiply the issue. Many old women drink red wine, having been convinced that it is good for the heart. Others stick stubbornly to Chardonnay or vodka. Elders who used to drink caffeinated coffee switch reluctantly to decaf, and then to tea. Water-bottled, imported, marketed—is our culture's idealized thirst quencher.

Our medicalized culture glorifies the drinking of water and the cutting-back of salt, although each can be too much of a good thing. All of us, at all ages, are told to drink water rather than sugary drinks such as cola or calorie-free drinks such as diet cola. Water is the goddess of the new age, although somehow it is best when it is bottled and imported from Fiji. In another irony of intake, old people may drink less water than the experts propose because of the consequences of drinking water. If we drink water, we have to go to the bathroom with greater frequency. So we cut back on drinking water, especially in the evening, so that we do not constantly have to get out of bed to pee, disturbing our partners or, possibly, falling and breaking a hip. Old people may be less likely than the young to feel thirsty, and they may cut back on drinking water so that they do not have to constantly go to the bathroom, especially at night (Brody, 2016).

Like sugary drinks, alcohol is contested terrain for the old (and young). Most of the old women drink alcohol; quite a few drink a lot. A few veterans of twelve-step programs do not drink at all. Some women give up alcohol on a temporary basis when they want to lose weight. Terry, 55, said that she had gained 70 pounds when she joined a sailing team and was not going to drink any more beer until she had lost those pounds. Iris says: "I really like to drink white wine. But I need to lose some weight, and when I want to lose weight I switch to vodka and don't drink wine; it's the carbohydrates."

The ingestion of alcohol into old bodies is getting considerable expert and media attention as of the mid-2000s, as is the ingestion of opioids. Legal rather than illegal substances are the choice of consciousness-altering substances among the old women, although "medical marijuana" makes an appearance both medicinally and otherwise. Eve asked Mandy if she was in pain; the answer was "yes." Eve said, "Aren't you still using those oils and brownies?" Annette said:

> I called Lily while I was away, and she was with Viola and Esther. They were laughing hysterically. When I asked them what was happening, Viola said she had got hold of some medical marijuana.

When alcohol or drug use is seen to go "too far," there are attempts to curb it, often by the spouse. Rosie asks her husband if she can have a second or third drink, while Candy's husband watches her to make sure that she does not have more than one or at most two glasses of wine. Friends can also serve as monitors. Lily, when she was in her fifties, confessed to a close friend that "I am taking too many opiates, and I have to stop." The friend threw her remaining pills into the toilet and helped with three days of severe withdrawal symptoms. By the mid-2000s, the use and abuse of alcohol and prescription drugs was framed in the media as a major medical and social problem for both the middle aged and the old (young people were also taken with heroin and crack cocaine, among other illegal drugs). There were attempts to clamp down on physicians' prescribing of painkillers, especially for old patients. For a few old women, there are self-help groups and rehab for ingestion practices that are labeled "addiction."

What goes in, must come out, so that the urinary and excretory systems of the old woman are at issue. These systems are in close proximity to the woman's sexual and reproductive organs. From youth, we women have been warned to wipe the anus in a direction opposite to our urinary and vaginal openings and to urinate and wash after sexual intercourse—or we run the risk of vaginal or urinary infections. For some of the old women, this is a never-ending cycle. Alice says "I have had a urinary infection for six months. They give me one antibiotic after another, and it just comes back." The marketplace is ready for us. Although freestanding bidets are uncommon in this country, some toilets feature genital-washing devices. In the absence of these features, the marketplace can sell us all kinds of wet wipes. Pharma can supply us over-the-counter pills for the pain of urinary infections and prescription antibiotics for vaginal and urinary infections.

The pharmaceuticals prescribed for old people for vaginal or urinary infections can interact with other pills they are taking to mimic psychiatric conditions, including dementia. Celia, 86, was committed to a psychiatric hospital with hallucinations and delusions. After several weeks her symptoms were traced to a combination of a UTI prescription with the multiple pain medications she was taking. She was released from the hospital free of psychiatric symptoms. These psychiatric "mimicking" problems are not limited to UTIs. Carol was taken to the ER for hallucinations and delusions after dental work in her upper jaw; the diagnosis was lidocaine psychosis, something that could have happened at any age.

Urinary incontinence afflicts many of the old women, from occasional leaking to missing the toilet by a few feet to the necessity for adult diapers at all times. More women than men have some degree of urinary incontinence, and more old women, by percentage, than young women. Using multiple data sources, the CDC estimates that more than half the women over 65 who are living in their own homes report some degree of urinary leakage (www.cdc.gov p. 5). Types of incontinence include stress incontinence, caused by laughing or coughing, and urge incontinence: not being able to hold urine long enough to make it to the toilet. Among the causes of incontinence is childbirth, which can afflict mothers of any age. Infections and illness can cause temporary incontinence. Carol wore her first Depends (sent free as a trial) during treatment for a urinary tract infection (UTI), and it was a bizarre and shocking experience. This episode of incontinence went away, but the other free trial Depends remain in the drawer, just in case.

The old women approach the problems associated with urination in various ways. Some wear protective pads, others adult diapers, and still others "pee pants" that feature a padded crotch. Sylvia, deceased at 69, wore adult diapers constantly for the last five years, saying that she sprayed urine when she laughed or coughed. Although some women feel ashamed of wearing diapers, Sylvia talked about it freely; the extra diaper that she always carried was visible when she opened her handbag. Humor, too, can dissipate shame. Norma, when an 85-year-old woman's incontinence was under discussion—they were planning a car trip to Las Vegas—said, "I am incontinent, we are all incontinent, so what? We don't have to stop on the way." Much laughter.

In addition to protective underwear, there are medical interventions for incontinence, including drugs, patches, and procedures. Lee, 87, who has urge incontinence, says that "As I age I have had an overactive bladder. I have used patches and medications . . . unfortunately they have caused constipation; therefore I have had to change my diet." One old woman describes two procedures to treat stress incontinence, offered at a local women's pelvic medical center:

> The injection I had is referred to as a urethral bulking agent. When I had it done before, collagen was used, but has since become unavailable and they have switched to Marcoplastique. The procedure takes about 30 minutes, requires anesthesia and a few hours in recovery. About 60–70% successful; many women need a follow-up injection. You can resume regular activities in a couple of days but no heavy lifting, etc. The urethral sling is more permanent but a more extended type of surgery.

In addition to pharmaceutical and medical interventions, there is a flourishing marketplace for adult incontinence products (and for the advertising thereof). While researching this article on her PC, Carol took a look at the major purveyors of adult diapers, pads and underwear. For months afterward, she was faced with pop-up advertisements every time she logged on to her computer. What is ironic about these ads is that all the people in them were youthful and slender, in their thirties and forties—despite the lesser prevalence of urinary incontinence among women aged 15–64 (www.cdc.gov p. 5). A few of the ads are for the traditional white adult diapers. But others feature "slim line, low rise" incontinence underpants in black or beige. Some of the ads depict young women in their twenties or thirties, wearing incontinence underwear while doing yoga or walking the streets holding hands. One features a middle-aged black man with two small children. In yet another, A young, buff man poses in snug gray incontinence tighties, his muscles bulging in a beefcake pose.

Somehow, incontinence advertising migrated from Carol's PC to Kathi's iMac. There are several brands of "pee pants," which, as indicated, have pads built in to the underpants, which then can be laundered like regular underwear. One brand of pee pants indicates the number of tablespoons of urine that their products can contain, ranging from 3 to 8. This brand uses, for its advertising to the old women, slender, youthful female torsos posing with several styles and colors of pee pants, from lavender to black and from a matronly to a bikini cut. Perhaps the advertisers think we old women will feel better if our incontinence role models are youthful and attractive.

Incontinence of feces ranges from minor incidents such as an error in judgment while passing gas to massive diarrhea. Fecal incontinence is less common than urinary, and there are no significant differences between men and women. About a fifth of noninstitutionalized people report some degree of fecal incontinence (www.cdc.gov p. 8). Serious incontinence—together with falls—is one of the major reason that old people are moved from their own homes into residential facilities.

> We are at the bar. Phyllis and Joe come through the door, they are both about seventy. Joe is in a wheelchair; he says "hello" in a sort of mumbly way. Later, as I pass Joe, I smell feces. Viola says, "He must have pooped." Soon thereafter Phyllis wheels Joe out of the room at a fair clip. . . . Later she told Kathi that she was going to have to get a caregiver for Joe because she could no longer move him around or deal with his fecal incontinence.

Joe's fecal incontinence was temporary and intermittent; he remains at home. Brian, who is now deceased, was moved from home into a nursing facility when he became fecally incontinent. Serious incontinence of feces is not only a major caregiving problem, it can also be very expensive. Brian, whose assisted living facility cost $3,300 a month when he was 70, was going through almost $1,000 a month of adult diapers, in part because of repeated episodes of diarrhea. The expense of disposable diapers is not limited to individuals and their caregivers, however. The image of our landfills as they bulge with the diapers of infants to 100-year-olds is a daunting one.

Some of the old women are willing to discuss urinary incontinence and how they cope with it, but what goes on in the households of old people who have temporary or intermittent problems with fecal containment is not well known. Illnesses such as food poisoning, together with many different medications, can cause diarrhea; in turn, diarrhea may not be as controllable among the elderly as it is among young adults. One 80-year-old woman's husband mentioned that she was having episodes of "slippage" during a nasty bout of intestinal distress. Problems with hygiene can occur when messy bowel movements—perhaps resulting from a poor diet—combine with the difficulties of arthritic hands cleansing the body thoroughly. These issues of hygiene are humiliating enough for old people; having to wear diapers is the final indignity. The anus, indeed, may be the part of the body of which we are most ashamed, disgusted and humiliated by as we age. So it is a relief to move on to something more ethereal—to every breath we take.

Animating our bodies in motion, from skeleton to skin, is the steady inhalation and exhalation of our breath. Breathing problems can occur at any age, and they can come and go but can be exacerbated over time. Carol has had asthma and chronic bronchitis since childhood—but pneumonia only since the age of 65. As we age, our ribcage bones may thin and change shape, and the diaphragm muscle may weaken. Lung tissue ceases to function as effectively as in earlier decades, and our immune systems suffer the same fate. Among the consequences of these changes are sleep apnea and a greater likelihood of asthma attacks, bronchitis, pneumonia and other lung issues. We, and those who live with us, are exhorted to pay attention to the breathing of the body. Carol learned, in her sixties, that if she cannot walk and talk at the same time she should get checked for pneumonia. She has been right several times during her early seventies.

Women who smoked cigarettes are liable to see the effects on their facial skin, especially the upper lip. Many of the old women did smoke when they were young, in the decades of the 1940s–1970s, when smoking was considered both sophisticated and harmless; Kathi was one of them, while Carol was not. Of all the hundreds of old women whose voices are heard in this book, only three (so far as we know) still smoked by the time they were 60. Sylvia was one of them; she died at 69 of lung cancer and other conditions. Casey, a chain smoker—who told us that learning to smoke was required by her college sorority—died of emphysema at 66. Tiffany, defiant at 68, smokes incessantly despite the grumblings of her husband and others.

Medical and recreation marijuana may be smoked or consumed. A few of the old women smoke marijuana recreationally (although they may obtain it medically), while others smoke it in the hope of getting some relief from pain. Some of the old women smoked a lot of marijuana in their youth but do so now either rarely or never. Others did not smoke until they were old, when they were prescribed marijuana to be eaten or smoked in cigarette or vapor form. Before her assisted suicide, Mandy, then 84, consumed marijuana brownies to relieve the pain of arthritis. Laura says that her 87-year-old mother was shocked when her doctor suggested the idea of smoking marijuana to relieve neuropathy pain in her feet, but "I dragged her to a pot shop and made her buy some"; Laura reported that it brought some relief to her mother. The effect of smoking tobacco on lungs old and young is well known; the effect of marijuana smoke or vapor much less so.

Our breathing bodies are in motion, inside and out, from throughout the decades from 60 to 100. If we are lucky—as we old women are lucky—our bodies can continue to function, with or without assistance, in our own homes. The transition from our own home to a residential home often comes about when one or more of the following conditions obtain: the old woman is incontinent, she is bed or wheelchair bound or she has been falling. Norma fell over her small dog, breaking her hip, an episode that precipitated a chain reaction of hospitalization and illnesses. She emerged from the hospital after three months, walking into her home despite the original prognosis "You will never walk again." May, 75, fell over a throw rug in her home, bringing about five months of hospitalization and treatment. Although she is back home, she is afflicted with various physical and emotional disabilities that she did not have before. Eventually Norma and her husband moved into an ALF, but May is still at home.

As we said earlier in this book, most of the old people prize being at home and do not want to move into the sequence of independent to assisted to memory care facilities. But there are a few—even privileged ones—who embrace the opportunities afforded by assisted living. Ella, 92, and her husband, Glenn, both enjoy their lives. They take advantage of all the opportunities offered by the ALF—trips to restaurants, stores, plays and movies—and love having others cook and clean for them. Their lives are full of friendship, family, love and laughter. Their son and daughter-in-law take them out every week for boating, a trip to the horse races, or to dinner and a movie. Although they have the various kinds of pain and stiffness associated with old age, their bodies remain in motion as they move through the world.

Most of us came of age in a time of bodily liberation both sporting and sexual: in the era of *Our Bodies Ourselves* we took joy in touch, sex, food, drink, marijuana, skiing, the heady scent of bodies. From skin to skeleton we are naked. We can see, and intimate others can see, the curve of our spine, the blotching of hands, the sagging of the flesh. Our digestive and urinary systems are our private business; our sexuality may be shared or unshared with another/others. But as we go about our days we reveal aspects of our bodies: height, weight, clothing, head, hands, feet—and perhaps other parts—arms, legs, navels, cleavage. Our public bodies are observed in outline, and from head to toe, the topic of the second part.

3
BRAIN AND SENSE
The Pains and Pleasures of the Flesh

Feelings of pleasure and pain are the touchstones of the sensate body, and we have felt these feelings throughout our lives. There is pleasure in beautiful sights, in wonderful sounds, in caresses, in a cool glass of water, in a glorious meal, in the scent of the ocean. There is pain in loss, in decay, in a headache or a stomachache. Over time, the pace and intensity of pleasure may erode, in part because of pain—the aged body's inheritor—and in part because of our fears of pain and death. In our youth, if we are healthy in mind and body, pleasure overwhelms pain. In old age, pain encroaches upon pleasure. But some of the pleasures of the flesh can remain throughout a lifetime.

We feel pleasure and pain through the brain and through the senses. Our bodies have five senses: touch, taste, smell, sight and hearing, corresponding to five sets of organs: skin, tongue, nose, eyes and ears. Our brains process these senses and store memories. Even by 50, we are not what we were, our brain or sense:

> Sixty is not the new 40. . . . Your sight has been getting worse, your other senses, too, and this, along with your ability to integrate information you are absorbing and then issue motor commands, means your balance is not what it used to be. . . . Your prefrontal cortex—where the concentrating and deciding gets done—has been shrinking for some time, perhaps since you graduated from

college. Do not kid yourself. . . . You are milling in the anteroom of the aged.

(Marzorati, 2016: 1)

Once out of the anteroom of old age into its main parlor, problems with the senses multiply. The lament of old age, its body, brain and sense, goes back many centuries; Maximianus, around 550 CE, complains:

Jealous old age, reluctant to hasten my end
Why come a laggard in this my worn-out body?
Set free my wretched life from such a prison.
Now hearing is less, taste less, my very eyes
Grow dim, I barely know the things I touch.
No smell is sweet, no pleasure now is grateful.
Devoid of feeling, who's sure that he survives?

(1988: 319–322)

The old women concur. Simone de Beauvoir (1972: 27) says that with aging

The sense organs are affected. The power of visual accommodation diminishes, the sight becomes less keen . . . the hearing as well. . . . Touch, taste and smell are all less sensitive than they were.

After she turned 70, Kathi's primary physician gave her a printout titled: "Adult Health Exam (Female), 70–79 Years: What is Happening at this Stage?" It informed her that

You have probably noticed physical changes that come from living a long time.
Your hair, skin and nails are thinner, drier, and more fragile.
It's easier to get cuts and bruises, and bruises can be larger.
You probably have wrinkles and age spots. . . .
You may have lost at least 2 inches from your usual height.

You may have lost muscle strength if you do not exercise. . . .

You may have stiffness and pain in your joints.

You may notice that your memory for little things is not quite as good, although your memories of past events are still strong.

You probably cannot see as well at night or dim light.

You may have cataracts.

You may notice that your eyelids are droopy and that your eyes are watery and dry.

Your hearing may not be quite as good. . . .

Your mouth may seem dry. . . .

Your bowels have probably slowed down a bit.

You may have problems with urinating.

You may not sleep as soundly as when you were younger.

You probably don't "bounce back'" from illness or injury quite as fast.

The upside—and there's not too much upside:

If you don't already have heart and lung disease or smoke, your heart and lungs probably work very well. You may still have a satisfying sex life.

We found this listing intriguing, so we asked for the 60–69 and 80 and over handouts. They are both about a third of the length of the 70–79 handout, confirming our sense that for most people the major bodily changes begin in their seventies. The first two sentences of the 60–69 handout captured our experience of our sixties perfectly: "Many women continue to enjoy good health in their 60s. This can be a time of great change." At 60, we were still young. By 69, we were not. In our sixties, we can expect that "it is easier to gain and harder to lose excess weight" and "Problems with constipation and with leaking urine are common." As in our next decade, the upside is that "You may still have a satisfying sex life."

By 80, the handout states that you may have gained weight but may have also lost up to 2 inches in height. The problems of skin to skeleton developing in your seventies continue to annoy. Memory problems are exacerbated, and you may not hear or see very well. You don't sleep soundly, and you don't "bounce back" as easily from illness or accidents. "The good news"—you guessed it—"You may still have a satisfying sex life." Plus, "your heart and lungs probably work as well as ever," and "A healthy woman in her 80s can expect to live into her 90s."

Throughout the lifespan, the senses are dependent upon the brain, and the brain upon the senses. We experience brain and sense as thoughts and feelings; seeing and hearing; reading; conversing; sleeping and dreaming, as our bodies move and function—breathing until we breathe and move no more. Although we old women are not anatomists or scientists, we have some idea of how our brains and our senses work within our bodies, and we watch and listen to our loved ones as they age in brain and sense. And we agree with those experts who tell us that as we age, our brain and senses are not what they were when we were young. We tap along with a cane, perhaps, wearing trifocals and hearing aids, the props of old age—but we still tap along, moving through and with the world.

Our brains can be affected at any age by medical conditions such as brain tumors. Other medical conditions, like the dementias, are linked to aging. There are a number of old women (and our spouses and partners) who have been diagnosed with dementias, but there are many more of us who are concerned about our memories. We worry when we cannot find our keys, retrieve someone's name, or remember what day of the week it is. We think about visiting the doctor to have some tests done, but then we reassure ourselves that we used to lose our keys even more frequently when we were younger, we have always been bad with names, and there is no reason, when retired, to know what day of the week it is.

Kathi: "Well I could not find my keys, but that's not as bad as Iris who was looking for her tennis shoes and they were on her feet!"

Carol: "I left the house the other day with two unmatched sandals on my feet. I said to myself, 'Oh no!' but then I reassured myself that I had done the same thing when I was in my mid-thirties."

We seek to retain our memory deficits within the ordinariness of everyday life rather than enter the terrain of a medical diagnosis. We want to contain our aging self within our old self, rather than accede to a new self with a brain and memory disease.

For those eventually diagnosed with a dementia such as Alzheimer's, there may come a critical moment of recognition. Geri Taylor was in her late sixties when she experienced that moment:

> It began with what she saw in the bathroom mirror . . . . [She] padded into the shiny bathroom of her Manhattan apartment. She casually checked her reflection in the mirror . . . . Immediately she stiffened with fright. Huh? What? She didn't recognize herself.
>
> (Kleinfield, 2016: 2)

Soon after this event, Geri went to a neurologist and received a diagnosis of "mild cognitive impairment, a common precursor" of Alzheimer's (Kleinfield, 2016: 2).

Fear of dementia stalks the old, perhaps more than despair over the aging body. But unlike the aging body—which is the subject of constant discourse among friends as well as family—dementia fears are often kept to oneself or shared only with spouses or partners.

Annette: "I worry about losing my mind, and I worry about Jan. I notice slips that we both make and wonder if it is just everyday forgetfulness or slipping into dementia. Jan worries about exactly the same thing."

Old people whose bodies are no longer themselves may be consoled by aspects of brain or sense that are not afflicted. Lee says that her 90-year-old husband is still "bright" despite his pain and use of a walker and that neither of them have had problems with dementia. The old ladies say, among themselves, "Whatever happens to our bodies, we hope our brains do not go." The bodily pleasures are diminished in old age, so we hope, like Lee, that our mental pleasures remain.

But bodily and mental pleasure is threatened by pain, which for many of us increases as we age.

Both pleasure and pain are experienced by the senses: sight, hearing taste, smell, and touch. Premodern philosophers wrote a lot over the centuries of Western culture about the senses and their hierarchy—which of the senses is the most important?—and by implication, which is the worst to lose. Aristotle put sight at the top of the hierarchy; contemporary researchers have documented that people in many cultures value vision over the other senses. For the old women, it depends. Some aspects of the senses are individual, such as the taste of food. Others, such as sight and hearing, have social and relational dimensions. Someone who has made her living and avocation through art or photography may privilege sight; a violinist, hearing. Couples whose relationship is deeply embedded in conversation might mourn the loss of speech (not a sense, but vital to communication), or hearing or a lack of feeling in the hands.

The organs of sense are the eyes, ears, nose, fingers and skin—all of which have both cosmetic and functional implications for aging bodies. Most organs shrink or at least stop growing in old age; the tongue and the external parts of the nose and ears continue growing. Drooping eyelids or earlobes, hairy nostrils, and thinning lips are all of concern to the old woman, even if the organs are still perfectly functional. Annette says: "I love earrings, but my earlobes are stretched and I don't want to stretch them anymore." Although the tongue has been the subject of (somewhat inexplicable) hilarity since ancient times, it is not an organ seen to need cosmetic surgery. But the other functioning sense organs are subject to medical and cosmetic intervention in the marketplace. Glasses, contact lenses and various surgeries modify sight, for the young as well as for the old. Surgeries and hearing aids restore some hearing. Drooping eyelids are raised up by cosmetic procedures, while earlobes can be clipped.

Sight is the preeminently social sense, by which we see at the moment we are seen. We express social judgment with our eyes and personal desire. Movements of the eyes are the first layer of social disapproval and control (Warren, 2011). When somebody has too many coupons in the grocery line, we see them, and we roll our eyes. When an old woman dresses too youthfully, we look at her with narrowed eyes and turn our head. But we also express desire and promise with the eyes. We flirt with the beautiful woman at the bus stop by a repeated, admiring glance—we cannot stare, because a fixed glance is socially inept. With dimmed sight, we lose possibilities of expression and participation. This is also true of hearing. A whisper of admiration, a sniff of disapproval, a sotto voce comment or a soft laugh cannot be heard by those who are going deaf.

Sight depends upon the eyes, the windows of the soul. The eyes of youth are brown and blue, gray, green and hazel, surrounded by white. In old age, our colors may still be bright and our look expressive, but the whites may be yellowed or bloodshot. Functionally, our eyes develop all kinds of issues as we age, starting with near- and farsightedness. Technological assistance for the near- or farsighted eyes—at any age— began with glasses, which were invented in the fourteenth century and were at first available only to the wealthy. We old women are willing to wear sunglasses because they could either be prescription or not, nobody knows. But prescription glasses are a different kettle of fish. Although prescription glasses are not exclusively an old age prop, women who did not need glasses when they were younger may balk at wearing them as they age. Many are willing, and some able, to wear contact lenses, although by the age of 70 or 80 contacts have sometimes worn out their welcome in the eye. Several wear neither prescription glasses or contact lenses and say, as Jolene, Carol and Eve do, "I just stumble around not seeing much."

> Amelia walks into the party, her glasses on so she does not trip. After she gets a drink and finds a table, she takes her glasses off and sets them down. When Rae points something out to her a few feet away, she puts on her glasses to take a look. Iris comes by to take a photo, and Amelia takes off her glasses and puts them down.

Medical/cosmetic interventions into the eye include laser surgery and cataract surgery. Women of all ages have tried laser surgery, hoping that it will improve their eyesight enough to avoid glasses or contact lenses. Cataracts come with aging eyes. If the old woman is 65 or older and requires cataract surgery, Medicare (as of this writing) pays. If someone younger wants or needs the surgery, they will have to pay out of their own pocket. Because cataract surgery can improve vision, people in their fifties and sixties pay for the surgery in order to see better.

Rae is sitting at the bar: "I just had my eyes done, it is great! I don't need glasses anymore." She explained that one eye had been altered to see reading material, and the other was for distance vision. The ophthalmologist who performs the procedure may give the old person options for how to modify their sight depending on what she wants to see the most: books, screens, or the traffic. We asked Rae if it hurt; she said no, "but the eye drops are bothersome." Ruby had the surgery when she was 75, and said, "I have not had to wear glasses since." Carol recently learned that she has a cataract in her left eye, and her optometrist recommended surgery as a safe and necessary procedure. When she told a friend this, the friend said, "My sister lost her eye to cataract surgery." So Carol is putting off cataract surgery for now.

Sight can begin to fail in early, middle or later life, requiring the services of optometrists. We turn to ophthalmologists when our eyes have problems beyond seeing so badly that we stumble around. Both of us have pterygia of the left eye, a visible pimple-like coating that covers part of the lens, apparently caused by sun exposure in earlier years. We also both have "floaters" of the right eye; they look like dust specks but they cannot be washed out—as Kathi's son, an optometrist, says: "Your chances of having a floater in your eye is a percentage equal to your age"—70% at 70, 90% at 90.

Conditions such as glaucoma and macular degeneration also afflict the old women, progressively limiting and eliminating the activities that once constituted the moving, everyday life self. Clarice, who has macular degeneration, says,

> "I used to be a great tennis player, I loved it. My arms were really muscular, and the right arm was bigger than the left. Then I had to stop playing tennis because I could not see."

Until recently, Clarice was one of Carol's regular internet Words with Friends players, usually winning. But now:

"I can't do it anymore. I have been playing with the enhanced system for the vision impaired, but it hurts so much that I can't do it."

Whenever we see Clarice and her husband she has a smile on her face and greets us by name. We ask her, "How do you know who we are?" She says "I recognize the height and shape of people."

The eyes have cosmetic as well as functional aspects, mediated by culture and the marketplace. There are many people—young and old, women and men—who do not want to wear glasses. As Casey put it when she was 60, "I don't want to go around looking at the world through frames." Women who wear contact lenses when they are young sometimes find that they cannot wear them decades later either because they are less adept at inserting or removing them or because they are causing discomfort. Some old women start wearing contact lenses for the first time in the years between menopause and 100.

After years of wearing glasses for reading and sports, Kathi, when she was 66, decided to get fitted for contact lenses. "I had tried to be fitted for them in my early 40s, when my vision changed, but due to an astigmatism, contacts were not an option for me." The primary impetus for getting contacts was the impending wedding of her daughter, but she also noted that wearing and changing and maintaining glasses had become a hassle, not to mention the fact that she thought that glasses made her look old. Learning to wear contacts for the first time at 66 turned out to be both challenging and more than a bit uncomfortable. Acquiring the skill of introducing a foreign object into the eye was not only difficult, it was somewhat painful. However, with the encouragement and support of her optometrist son, the switch to contacts was completed in about two weeks' time.

Contact lenses, as well as improving sight, can be colorful; some women have experimented with different-colored eyes, although usually at an earlier age. Joan, who is in her mid-fifties, says changing eye color "is just for fun, like lipstick or something. My eyes are brown, and I have had them green and blue." Others have enhanced their eye color indirectly, with eye makeup, since their youth, and may continue to do so: eyeshadow, eyeliner, under-eye liner, mascara or false eyelashes.

Eye makeup is removed at night (if the old woman is not lazy) and replaced by various eyelid and under-eye cream. The ritual begins the next morning, because the eyes are the windows of the soul, and the center of the face, as well as the organ of sight.

Our ears shelter the organs of hearing, which can become afflicted as the decades pass. Tinnitus, hyperacusis and partial or total deafness all have an effect on the hearing sense. Tinnitus—hearing ringing, hissing or other sounds inside the ear—can occur at any age but is more likely among older people because it is associated with a loss of hearing. Kathi developed tinnitus at the age of 69; her audiologist told her that in her case there is no loss of hearing. There is also not much to do about the problem, aside from playing music with earphones or trying to ignore it. Kathi says: "It is not so troublesome when I am doing something, distracted by something, or watching TV. It is in those moments of quiet that it is really most annoying."

Many of the old women we know cannot hear very well and thus are partially deaf. Esther, who had rubella during her childhood, has been deaf in one ear since that time, while other old women have problems in both ears. Hearing aids are one of the "props" of old age that many old women will not use; Esther refuses to use one, and so does Lillian, in her eighties. Lillian's children determined that she was hard of hearing and bought her a hearing aid, but she was, in her sister's words, "too stubborn" to wear it; "she thinks there is nothing wrong with her." The old woman with one good ear turns it toward the voice; the hard of hearing old woman smiles and nods, the conversation abuzz around her. Kathi tells Carol that she needs a hearing test pointing out that "What did you say?" has become a frequent part of daily conversation; Carol says that she does not need to be tested. Carol wonders if her hearing is OK or if she is in denial and needs a hearing test.

Deafness shuts out the subtleties of social interaction and the ways of everyday life. Ruby says that her husband is hard of hearing. "It makes it very difficult to have a conversation. He answers questions that I have not asked, but he doesn't answer questions that I have asked." Deafness and blindness also shut off the world beyond our households. We have libraries, art galleries and operas as we have had for centuries; we now have the visual media from television to the internet. Sights and sounds swirl around us, but we cannot participate in them. Ruby says that she and her husband used to have season tickets to the theater and symphony, but "we don't anymore because he can't hear." Alice and Mac stopped going to the local bar for weekly team trivia because, as she said a few months before he died, "Mac can't hear any more, and he doesn't enjoy it."

The opposite problem is hyperacusis, or hearing too much sound, an uncommon condition that affects all ages. Carol was first diagnosed as having too much auditory response when she was in her thirties. It is not a problem equivalent to deafness, just annoying: "Someone banging around in the kitchen when I am sitting in the living room sets my teeth on edge. If I am IN the kitchen I am likely to cover my ears or leave the room." Compared with deafness, hyperacusis is a mild and minor problem of the old or young.

We hear, and we speak, and we vocalize. Some vocalizing is seen as "normal" for young and old people: a whistle to a dog, a snatch of humming, an occasional "tsk." But then there are the seemingly random vocalizations of old age. There is blog after blog on the internet filled with relatives and caregivers complaining about the various noises made by old people throughout the day, from "hrumph" to a clicking tongue. The old person may or may not realize that they are vocalizing. Lay explanations for these old people's vocalizations include deafness, anxiety, dementia and filling the silence. Old people are expected to talk, not grunt, as they interact with others. Kathi and Carol, over the past year, have both noticed the other making random noises, and, like nothearing, this has become one of the issues of mutual aging.

Speech is vital to communication with family, friends and strangers, unless one knows sign language. Although some of the women in this book reached us, by request, through emails and mail, most swirled around us in the conversations of everyday life, with each other and with our friends and acquaintances. Ruby can no longer communicate successfully with her husband because of his deafness, and not because he has become unable to speak. We old people should be grateful, we suppose, that muteness does not develop with old age along with deafness and blindness. But there is the silence of dementia.

Over the past decade we have seen the silence of dementia descend, bit by bit, upon some of the people we know. There are several everyday indicators of the possibility of dementia, readable by those around the old person. She or he may get more voluble, even swearing and shouting—Carol's mother did, close to the time of her death. But in the early days of dementia, the old person who finds herself not tracking the conversations swirling around her may fall silent, not wanting to seem out of touch or confused. There is a considerable "how to handle" body of advice on attempting to restore the voices of those who have fallen silent through dementia. Kontos (2015: 178) says that cultural—as opposed to neurological—understandings of dementia frame it as "an experience through which nature, history, culture, power and discourse all speak simultaneously."

Sight, hearing and talk are preeminently social. Taste and smell have social implications, but they are the provenance of the individual body as we move around in the world. As we age, the senses that govern eating and drinking become less powerful. This can be a boon in a nursing home filled with the unpleasant odors of overcooked cabbage, urine and disinfectant, and where the meals are unpleasant to look at and to eat. But in the everyday lives of old women, the diminution of the taste and smell of good food can be saddening, especially when they have felt pride in their cooking (Warren and Williams, 2008). The old women were often the preparers as well as the tasters of meals, with their pride in cooking and feeding their family good things tied together with their sense of self; women in residential facilities lament their inability to cook, nurture their families with home-cooked meals, and enjoy their own food (Warren and Williams, 2008). On the other hand, old women who are not in residential facilities may grow tired of cooking for their families because of failing health or feeling worn out from gendered chores.

Laura: "My son and his family are coming for the holidays, with their children and my daughter-in-law's parents. I don't want to have to cook for all those people for a week, but I don't want to have to go out and eat either. It is so expensive, and the food is not always good." We agree, and we all sigh—and laugh.

Smell and taste are intertwined with each other, inhabiting the nose and tongue. There are five tastes: sweet, salty, sour, bitter and umami; two other candidates are soapy and metallic—both of which are claimed by people who can't abide the taste of cilantro. Adults have around a hundred thousand taste buds, which go through a two-week cycle of birth, death and regeneration, but after the age of 40 there is less and less regeneration (Park, 2014). So old people often look for more, not less, salt and spice in their food, contrary to some nursing home practices. Children given sugar often prefer sweetness, although there is usually a turn to salty later in life. Part of adult sensuality is the taste of things: an apple, a beer, a piece of chocolate. As we grow the sense of taste, as well as digestive issues and a lessened sense of smell, may diminish the enjoyment of food and drink.

Taste is in the mouth and nose; smell surrounds us through the nose and mouth. All kinds of scents come to us on the wind, diminished but not erased by old age. We smell the snow blown by the wind on a crisp winter night, or the sun on our arms as we sit on the beach. A perfume worn by a passer-by reminds us of our youth. The restaurant we love and frequent smells of freshly baked bread. We old women remain tethered to the world around us by smell as well as by taste, sight and hearing.

But smell is not only part of our surroundings, it comes to us from other bodies and from our own; others smell us and are smelled by us, we smell ourselves. One of the indignities of old age is incontinence of urine and/ or feces, discussed in the previous chapter in the context of diapers and underwear. Changing those diapers and underwear is a major olfactory challenge; along with falling, incontinence is one of the factors precipitating institutional placement of the elderly. Francie says of her husband: "I am going to have to place him soon if I can't find a caregiver; having to move him around and change his pants, these are too much for me."

Even among the continent, the old body may smell worse as the decades pass, either in parts of the body or the whole body through the skin. Viola says, "Of late I have been having trouble with my underarms; they smell. I shower just like I used to, and I use deodorant, but I still have BO." Annette responds: "I have the same problem, but for some reason my left underarm is worse!" We all laugh—the only remedy. The internet is full of comments about increasing genital odor in old women, one's own and others, and what to do about it—the bilgewater of elderly Timo's private parts.

There is a genetic condition, trimethylaminuria, that makes the entire body of the sufferer smell of rotting fish. Among the endless nutritional advice in today's world, we are told that we should eat fish—oily fish, for that matter, such as sardines and salmon. But eating fish can have the same effect, temporarily, as the fish disease has permanently. Both of us find that if we eat fish our skin exudes a fishy odor for a couple of days. So we don't eat fish often—with one exception. Smoked salmon, which we are privileged to be able to afford, does not cause an odor problem—at least for us, at least for now. Laura laughs at us: "Fish is good for you; now you are not eating fish!" We do not tell her why.

Among the ironies of old age is being unable or unwilling to consume or do things that are supposed to be good for you. We rarely eat fish because our bodies then smell of fish. We do not drink enough water because we do not want to be going to the bathroom all the time. Fruit and vegetables, supposed to be so good for you, are intestinally challenging. Pulse foods such as beans are pretty much out of the question. Not everything is good for everyone at every age. Spinach and blueberries are said to be good for your health. But Carol has been advised not to eat them—and many other fruits and vegetables—because one of the chemicals in them, oxalate, is implicated in kidney stones, which she has had on repeated occasions. At least the ancients judged the body's health by the four humors. Now we have one-size-fits all food recommendations by those "experts."

Old age has many smells beyond that of fish. Because incontinence affects old people more than young—especially old women—they may smell of urine or feces. They may not have the strength, or enough money, to keep up with contemporary standards of body, clothing and underwear hygiene. Young people pause at the door of an elderly couple, fearing a neglected and dirty house, old clothing and unwashed bodies—"mothballs and musty house" (Sifferlin, 2012). Old people who are too frail to do housework, or too poor to pay for it, may see their households become dirty. They do not replace upholstery, drapes, furniture and carpets. All grows decrepit and unclean.

Carol: "I went to the home of a retired professor in his nineties and his wife. The place was ancient, painted the kind of green we used to associate with lead paint and hospitals. The ceiling was festooned with cobwebs. He offered me tea, and I accepted—not really wanting it, because I had no idea if the teacups were clean."

But even the cleanest clothes, bodies and homes of old people may smell different than those of young people. According to a neuroscientist at the Monnell Chemical Senses Center in Philadelphia, old people:

have a distinct smell . . . [which] might be an evolutionary skill related to the way other animals are able to sniff out young, virile mates, and avoid those who are older.

(Sifferlin, 2012)

Old person smell is distinct from—and added on to—the environmental smell of facilities for the aged. Whether in Sweden or the United States, these facilities tend to smell like urine and the chemicals used to clean up the urine (Sifferlin, 2012).

The marketplace is ready for the battle against old person smell. The Japanese company Shisheido markets odor-masking products to quell what they call "Old Man Smell." These products range from a perfume for the old called "Odor" to "deodorant-coated men's suits" and a chewing "gum that causes fragrance to emanate from skin pores when chewed'" (Crockett, 2015). In Western culture, it is old women rather than old men who are odiferous.

Ovid: Thais smells worse than a fuller's pot, worse than an amphora spoilt with rotting brine . . . .
Horace: What a sweat, what a reek enwraps every part of her flabby limbs.

(de Beauvoir, 1972: 122)

Others smell us; we smell ourselves; we may not smell much else. As we will see in later chapters, incontinence issues in old age add to the tyranny of smell for the old body.

Even if we become sightless, deaf and without taste or smell, we are left with feeling and with touch, perhaps to the very end. An old woman who is deaf, mute and dumb can still feel the breeze across her body, or, if she has loved ones, the sense of a caress. But sensation itself can become distorted—that warm wind on our cheeks can start to feel cold. Our invisible system of blood circulation, part of our receptivity to hot and cold, changes over time. On a 70-degree day, Kathi said:

> "I saw the hundred-year-old woman today. She was sitting in her wheelchair in the garage, caregiver nowhere to be seen. She was bundled up and wearing mittens."

Or the old woman gets too hot and sweats. Long past menopause, some women in their seventies and eighties continue to experience hot flashes. Kathi still has them, typically at night, but she has noted that they are of lesser intensity and duration than those that accompanied menopause. Other old women report that they are constantly chilled, requiring an extra sweater or scarf to be comfortable while those younger folks around them are in shirtsleeves.

As her daughter pushes her 100-year-old mother around the street, she reaches down and touches her cheek. Touching and being touched involve skin—the breath of the wind on our cheeks, the kiss of a lover on our face, the grasp of a baby. Hands and fingers reach out and caress. But the sensation of touch may diminish with old age, and not only because of lessened sensitivity in fingers and skin. It is a truism of old age in isolation that what is missed most is the touch of another—which is one reason to have pets to snuggle up to. As Jolene said a few weeks after her husband died, "I reach over to snuggle with him in bed, and he is not there. So I go and look for my cat."

As women age, the balance of their sensations may shift from pleasures to pains. A number of the old women, including Jolene, struggle with physical pain day after day, month after month. Some pain becomes medicalized and treated: knees or hips are replaced, rheumatoid arthritis soothed with pills, achy muscles eased with analgesics. But there is a whole world of pain that shades between the medically diagnosed and the mysterious that afflicts us as we age. Pain comes in three sets of affliction: chronic to acute, mild to severe and permanent-frequent-fleeting. As we age, the likelihood of any combination of these pain axes increases, in more and more parts of the body. In his (rare) sociological exploration of pain, Kotarba (1983) says:

> Since it fits the overall experience of growing old, chronic pain is considerably less traumatic and problematic for the elderly than for the young.
>
> (p. 59)

Pain may be less traumatic for the old than for the young in the sense that it is less unexpected. But it can be equally traumatic in another way: as a harbinger and reminder of decline and death. And pain is problematic for the young and for the old in different ways. For the young, it is an interference with the life of youth: with participation, sports, dating, moving around in the world. For the old it is part of the drawing-in of experience away from the outside into the center of identity—that of an old person, an old body.

Pain occurs in the functioning systems of the old woman's edifice. Bone pain afflicts the skeleton, upper or lower back pain restricts motion and muscle pain stiffens the arms and legs. All the functioning systems are sites of pain: the digestive, the urinary and the reproductive/genital. Even the skin hurts when some conditions are present. The causes of pain are many and varied, including illness, injury, over-exertion, exposure to toxins, allergens and ingestion of contaminated food or drink. Some pains—such as constipation or the cramps of diarrhea—may go away of their own accord, while others, especially those affecting movement, may not be so fleeting. Back, knee and hip pain among the old women, and shoulder pain among old men who used to play football, prompt the seeking of medical attention. Our joints are out of joint; cartilage wears out, our tendons ache with tendonitis and those little bursa sacs that cushion our joints get inflamed.

There is a nexus of pleasure and pain in drugs, both legal and illegal, and even some nostalgia. Wilma, 80, says that she and her husband "grew marijuana plants in the yard, by the fence so they could not be seen."

Kathi: "You could grow them again now if you wanted."
Wilma: "Yes, we could, but we don't want to, it is not the same, nothing is the same." Sighs and laughter.

In our youth, for some of us, illegal and legal drugs gave us pleasure. In our old age, this may still be true for some of us, but no longer for others. Some old women have been using marijuana for decades, initially for pleasure but in recent years as medication for anxiety. We tease Mandy, 86, about the medical marijuana she uses for the pain of an auto-immune disease. Perhaps we take OxyContin for the rush of pleasure it gives us, perhaps for the deadening of intense pain that it brings us.

There are pills and injections for bodily pain, and there is also surgery. Severe, unremitting pain in the back, neck, hips or knees affects the functioning of the edifice; sufferers at first cannot play sports, but eventually they cannot even walk. Thus, many of the old women have had, or continue to have, surgeries of the joints—with varying outcomes. Nicole had an unsuccessful hip replacement followed by a repair; now—many months later—she walks without a cane and without pain. For Nicole, and for many others, these pain and repair trajectories are grueling, not only because of the pain but because outcomes are so variable over time. Louise spent weeks in bed with sciatic pain, unable to walk or sit for more than a few minutes. She says after her back surgery: "It is a new and improved pain. The sciatic pain that hurt so much and went down my legs is gone. The pain from the where they did the insert and the bone graft is hell." But both graft and incision pain eventually dissipated.

Perhaps the most pervasive of function-damaging pain for so many old women is arthritis. This disease has many types and takes many pain-forms, from mild to moderate to severe. When it is mild to moderate, the women may continue their activities, at least to some degree and perhaps with the assistance of over-the-counter pain relievers. Lee is typical: "I have arthritis. I have continual pain." When Eve winces as she gets into her golf cart, she does not say anything, but we know that her legs and arms are hurting. Both Lee and Eve say that they refuse to let pain curtail their activities or control their emotions.

Pain of all types, stages and degrees is depressing to the old women: chronic and acute, temporary and permanent, moderate or severe. It is depressing because it hurts, first of all; after that, it interferes with activities and provokes fear of further pain and ultimately the loss of self. Many agree that if we have our mental and physical health we would rather be alive, but that perhaps we would rather die if we don't have that health.

Carol: "My mother was deep into vascular dementia, she made no sense at all. Decades ago she had told me that in her bedside drawer was a lethal dose of pills and made me promise that I would give them to her if she ever lost her mind. During the flight to see her after my father's death I pondered this the whole way, knowing that I could not keep my promise. When I eventually arrived at the house, she looked at me as I came through the door, snapped right out of her dementia, and said, 'Your father would have wanted me to live,' then fell right back into her comatose state. And there were no pills in the bedside drawer."

Living with pain brings sadness in its wake, and the fear of decline and death. There is an enormous range of pleasurable and painful sensations and emotions possible to the body at any age, but those most associated with old age in Western culture are, in the words of Sir Francis Bacon in the thirteenth century: "Phlegmatic . . . Melancholy . . . fearful" (Oxford p. 35–35). A psychologist might call these anhedonia, depression, and anxiety or paranoia. Their everyday equivalents are a loss of pleasure, sadness and fear.

Old age often brings with it the slipping-away of enjoyment; not only are we not able to play tennis as often as we used to, but when we do it does not give us as much sheer physical pleasure as it did—especially if we are in pain with arthritis. The sensate may give us less pleasure. Eve says that "I used to love going to the beach and lying in the sun. Now I don't like the sun at all." Tennis is not as much fun as it used to be—and then we fall, or our knees start to hurt. We are afraid to try again because we are afraid of injury and more pain. Anhedonia, sadness, fear and pain wind us down, gradually, into stillness. The experts tell us that sitting is the new smoking, and we believe them, so we get up and go for a walk, which, as we saw in Chapter 2, is the last bastion of motion among the aged. And then, perhaps, we cannot walk at all. And we fall into melancholy.

"Geriatric depression" is the clinical condition; sadness is its everyday equivalent. Old women experience the sadness of loneliness, of loss and of bodily pleasure, health and strength. Jolene says, "Since Syl died, I don't know what to do with myself. I don't know where to go or even if I want to go anywhere. He was always the one who got us moving." We discuss, often, the depressing effect of illness as we age. Not only cancer but the "common cold" takes away parts of the days, weeks or months that we have left, reminding us of the old woman's trajectory of frailty. If we are alone, we have to cope; if we have partners or spouses, we are a burden on them, exposing them to viruses and the stresses of caregiving.

Both economic hardship and loneliness are more likely to affect old women than old men, in part because women have a lower net worth and in part because men are more likely to be partnered than old women (Spar, 2016). The women we know are not threatened by economic hardship, but they may be lonely. Among the aged, there is the loneliness of being truly alone, without (much of) a social network, and the loneliness of not being partnered, although within a social network. The women we know are not lonely in the first sense, but some of them are lonely in the second. Jolene says, wistfully, "It feels really weird having nobody, when I have had someone at my side for fifty years, and now he is not there. And I don't think there will be anyone else at my age."

Old men and women are fearful: of death, decline, loss and— increasingly—the bodily consequences of the activities of everyday life. We are walking with Doreen, 78, who is wobbling slowly behind us. She says, "Why am I afraid of everything?" Carol: "Because you are old." Doreen: "I am afraid of elevators, of escalators, of curbs, of walking. I am afraid I will trip and fall." Kathi suggests a cane; Doreen snorts. Despite the fear—and real probability—of falling, many of the old women, like Doreen—and Ella, whom we met earlier—will not use that signature prop of old age. The fear of looking old(er) trumps the fear of being older.

Many of the old women have driven cars since their youth—a few, tractors. Driving expands the terrain of bodily motion and gives a sense of freedom and speed that is part of both experience and the cultural landscape. Some of the oldest women are fearful that their right to drive will be taken away from them in the next year, at the next driving test. We all know the stories about old men and women who are still driving into their eighties and nineties and are involved in accidents and injuries. And we try to balance the old person's fear of losing her freedom against society's fear of impaired driving.

We hear the roaring of a Maserati outside our windows and know that it is either our 55-year-old neighbor, John, or our 80-year-old neighbor, Raoul, roaring up the street. Their wives drive the "other" car. Another neighbor Gilda, 78, drove to the supermarket and beauty parlor while her husband was still alive, while her husband did the driving when they traveled to see their adult children in other states. After he died, she wanted to continue driving but failed the driving test twice. She is resigned to not driving but misses the freedom and spontaneity of getting behind the wheel by herself. She can afford the services of a private driver, which sets her apart from the poor elderly.

We joke that Raoul and several of the other old men in the neighborhood dress in such a way that they do not appear to be Maserati owners—knit caps pulled low over their eyes; ragged T-shirts, torn and dirty jeans. The old women are more careful about their appearance; unlike their husbands, most of them do not want to look like bag ladies. The old women looked askance at Sylvia, who adopted (despite considerable wealth and an apparently intact mind) the trappings of the bag lady—toothlessness, raggedy hair, odd and mismatched clothing—and wonder how she can do this—and if this could happen to them. Nora Ephron (2006) describes her beauty and diet routine—hair, clothing, makeup, weight watching—and fears that if she lets up for one moment she will look like the bag lady she sees in the street.

A few of the old women fear not looking like but actually becoming the bag lady: poor, unkempt and homeless, without a family or a community. Bag lady fears seem particularly true for feminist old women. Gloria Steinem says that after 50 she began to worry about "ending up as a bag lady"; she "handled it by saying to myself, I'll organize the other bag ladies" (Steinem, 2015: 249). Schwartzbaum (2013) describes how the Woody Allen movie *Jasmine* embodies the fear of "so many feminist women I know . . . ending up as a bag lady . . . our darkest and clammiest fear"—poor, homeless, done, invisible, forgotten.

Some of the fearful, like Schwartzbaum, are single; others have partners whom they fear will leave them and take all their resources—or stay with them and use up all their resources. One feminist, commenting on Spar (2016), justifies face-lifts and tummy tucks for old women because by not staying youthful "they face losing a spouse, or a salary which can mean the difference between a home and homelessness" (Wertheim, 2016). Ruby, despite being well off, was fearful of the bag lady in her fifties when she was single. At 80 she has a husband who earns less than she does: "I have to pay for him if we do anything, if we take a cruise or go on a vacation. I have to pay most of the rent. He doesn't have a lot of money." Ruby was afraid that she would run out of money, spending it on both herself and her husband, and she refuses to become a bag lady.

Fear has psychological and psychiatric implications for a medicalized culture. We are officially, in the mid-2000s, living in the "Age of Anxiety," following the 1990s depressed "Prozac Nation." Antidepressant prescriptions have not declined, but anti-anxiety medications have escalated. Anxiety affects women and men of all ages, prompted by world conditions and events as well as inner turmoil. Bassil (2011: 65) notes that "there is a misconception that [anxiety] drastically declines with age." In old age, anxiety is often accompanied by depression and may be experienced somatically as pain. Although two-thirds of psychiatry patients with depressive disorder have their first diagnosis in the late teens to late twenties, one third are first diagnosed after age 50 (Bassil, 2011). Worry about world conditions and events can take on new life when grandchildren and great-grandchildren are born. Loss and grief can leave the old woman anxiously poised for the next loss, the next grief. And old age anxiety links with the other emotions of old age: it fuses with depression, moves fear towards phobia, and increases anhedonia. Rosie adds that until recently she has never been depressed, "but now I am always sad."

Paranoia is a special kind of fear involving what other people might be doing or saying. In its psychiatric shape, it is accompanied by hallucinations or delusions. But in its everyday form, the old person is afraid of what other people might be doing to or taking from her. Carol's mother, in her mid-eighties, believed that her long-time housekeeper and caregiver was taking her possessions. She was becoming forgetful of where she might have put her jewelry, keys or wallet at the same time as she was experiencing the bodily vulnerabilities of old age. At 85, there is no fighting back or fighting off. And when the old woman is removed to a new environment such as a nursing home, the strangeness of place and person often intensifies her fear of others.

Old men and old women may all be haunted by a loss of pleasure and by fear, melancholy and anxiety—even paranoia—but there are also gendered emotions as we age: the anger of men and the shame of women (of course, women can be angry and men ashamed, too). Women who are now 60 to 90 grew up in a time when men were supposed to be the breadwinner and care for wife and family, while women were supposed to be taken care of and look beautiful. For some of the old women and men none of this was true, but it was nevertheless a cultural context. Anger at losing their strength and preeminence is one male response to aging. Lee says of her husband that he is "very angry, which affects our relationship." For all old people there are several arenas of shame within the aging body, including but not limited to incontinence. In an article on what prevents old people from seeking treatment for urinary incontinence, the authors focus on shame. As one 68-year-old woman says

By the time I've got out of bed and just got round there . . . I thought "oh no," that's what makes you feel old and ashamed of yourself. I'm losing me.

(Horrocks et al., 2004: 695).

The shame of losing control of bodily functions is at the same time a sense of losing oneself. We can imagine an old man saying the same thing.

But there is a gendered shame for old women in contemporary Western culture: a comparative shame, in the context of an enormous weight of images and words. We have seen that unbearable weight brings shame to women—and men—throughout a lifetime. The TV series, "Grace and Frankie," shows Jane Fonda as a sexy blond, moving quickly through a charmed life—although she does have some incontinence, and difficulties keeping (although not acquiring) boyfriends. As Annette says, "If she can be like that, why can't I be like that?" She sighs and looks down.

> "It makes me feel bad, that I don't do enough, try harder. I am sure if I tried harder I could lose some weight, then my knees would not be so bad, then I would walk better and look better."

Shame also surrounds being unable to live up to media and medical exhortations to look young, keep fit; "Seventy is the new fifty" tells us 70-year-olds we had better look, and preferably feel, twenty years younger. Nora, who has held the appearance of old age at bay with numerous face- and body-lifts, is ashamed of the other depredations of aging. "I am slowing down," she says. "I can't help it. That is the way it is." She sighs and turns her head. She is also wistful, remembering how it used to be. She touches the beautiful skin of a woman of 50, and says, "how do you get your skin to be like that?" Shame about the present body, as well as wistfulness for the past body and for the body of the presently young, is a common feeling among the old women.

Humiliation is the public face of shame, for both men and women. An 83-year-old woman said that she worried about incontinence because others might find her unclean (Horrocks et al., 2004: 695). Old women in public, in residential facilities and at home with partners, spouses and family face humiliation as they attempt to control their bodily functions—farting, burping and fecal and urinary incontinence. Other old people experience the humiliation of falling or fainting in public.

Carol: "I fell at the club the other day, tripped over a concrete block and landed on my knees, which started to bleed a lot. Everyone stopped talking and turned to look at me. Several people rushed up with sympathy and suggestions—'Are you all right?' 'Don't get up.' I said, 'I am fine,' and got out of there."

Experiencing public humiliation makes the old woman feel embarrassed: I look old, I look drunk although I have not had a drink, I look foolish.

There are remedies for the unpleasant emotions of old age, of both the psyche and the body. Our medical culture ensures that our body is the site of remedy, in the shape of antidepressants and anti-anxiety medications to help us banish fear and a sense of loss; the marketplace encompasses both Big Pharma and the sites that sell self-help books for the aged. We, the old people, are told to live in ways that mix the positive into the negative: be sociable and kindly, helpful and involved, busy—at least, make sure we have some distractions. Go to the movies, gossip, play word games. And we are told to exercise as much as we can, to rest when we need to and to get enough sleep (but not too much—therein lies another signal of depression).

Sleep, which involves both brain and sense, is in paradoxical relation to them. To go to sleep both shuts off the senses and awakens them. Dreams and nightmares transport the sleeper across time, space, and relativity. The quantity and quality of sleep is a preoccupation of many old people and their families and caregivers. An adult is supposed to sleep through the night; an old person might be permitted a nap. But she is not expected to doze in the common room of a nursing home or fall asleep at the dining table. Old people become distressed when they cannot sleep or when they wake up routinely at 3 am. There are adults who claim to get by on, and thrive, with four or five hours' sleep a night. We two need eight or nine to function decently. Experts used to tell us that we need less sleep as we age; now they say we need the same amount as younger adults.

Many of the disorders of old age interfere with sleep. Overactive urinary systems interrupt our nights; as Eve says, "I get up several times a night to go to the bathroom." Bad knees preclude running or even walking, so that the tiredness that comes from exercise is absent. But even the healthy elderly may have more trouble with sleep than they did in earlier years. We are more light-sensitive. Ruby says that "I broke down and got blackout curtains" for her rented condo because the light coming in at 5 in the morning woke her up. For Kathi, entering her seventies was heralded by sleep disturbances; she sleeps for a couple of hours, wakes up for a bit, goes back to sleep . . . and so it goes. Couples may continue to sleep with one another even when the behavior of one person causes sleeplessness in the other. Vickie and Bill are in their early seventies.

Vicky: "I don't sleep very well because Bill is restless and wakes me up."
Kathi: "Well, you could sleep in separate beds."
Vicky: "No, then he would wake me up anyway, he would keep checking
　　to see if I am dead." Laughter.

Complaints of sleeplessness may prompt physicians to prescribe sleeping pills to the old women. Sleeping pills and other medications may cause hypersomnia—excessive sleeping, the reverse of insomnia. Laura says of her 90-year-old mother "She sleeps twenty hours a day. I don't know what is wrong with her. She may have to go to assisted living." According to Laura, her mother sleeps all through the night, then takes naps constantly throughout the day. Some old women find a nap during the day refreshing, and it does not interfere with their sleep. A 70-year-old who feels embarrassed to nap "like an old person" might fall asleep in the evening while watching television, then not be able to sleep through the night.

After a good sleep, and despite the multiple pains of the flesh, there are times we feel bodily pleasure, or at least well-being. Bernard Berenson (1994) asks: "At my age what is it to be happy?" He concludes that it is:

being relatively free from burning toes and finger tips, from a feeling of bloatedness, from stabbing aches and pains anywhere, from nausea and a disgusting taste in the mouth, from difficulties with bladder and intestine.

Happiness is sometimes framed, especially by the oldest old, not as pleasure but as absence: of problems with the functioning digestive and urinary systems (Berenson does not mention his Pecker), of disorders of the senses and the brain, and of pain.

Although it is the private body that feels pain, our pain affects the activities of our everyday life, as well as our spouses and partners (which we will discuss in Chapter 6). When we go out in public, we may demonstrate our pain bodily or through props such as canes or walkers. Louisa had back surgery a month before.

> Louisa comes into the restaurant with her husband, walking unassisted by walker or cane. They walk by us and Carol says "Lou"—she turns and walks over; halfway to our table she winces, and she seems to lose her footing for a moment.

Louisa later responds to an inquiry about her pain: "It is better than it was, I am on a lesser dose of opioids." Among the old women, we talk about it all. When we were young adults, we swore that we would never become the kind of old person who talks about our ailments. And now we are precisely that kind of old person. Pain is not only discussed, it is displayed in our body language and in our props: we wince, we scrunch up our eyes, we say "ouch," we limp into the room with a cane. We take our private bodies—skeleton to skin, brain and sense—into the world around us; here and there, now and then, they are our public bodies as well.

PART II
THE PUBLIC BODY

4

THE BODY OBSERVED

From Head to Toe

Whatever we old women look and feel like naked and in private, we have appearances to keep up in public. Our public body shows off not only its fat or thin outline, but (almost always) its head, face, hands (usually), feet (in warm climates) and (possibly) arms and legs, underarms and midriffs, elbows and knees. We may choose to cover our arms and legs, or not. Our heads, covered or bare, are the focus of the gaze of self and other: face, chin, hair, mouth, teeth—eyes, noses and ears too, the organs of our senses. Our hands and fingernails are visible to others and to ourselves most of the time. Our feet and toes are the bottom rung, observed in sandals or enclosed in footwear.

If the eyes are the windows of the soul, the face is its mirror. People look at our faces. Eyes make contact with eyes, and they assess facial expressions. They note the high cheekbones, and the smiling, full lips with their white teeth. For the sighted, people are recognized by their faces. As we age, our faces may remain the same, and we remain recognizable—especially if we keep the same hair color and style. But some women undergo changes that make their faces less recognizable from earlier decades. With weight gain, increase in fat deposits flatten the cheekbones and may produce a double chin. With weight loss, the cheekbones may become visible for the first time. Gravity also takes its toll on facial muscles and connective tissue. And then there are the old women's wrinkles.

The 60- to 90-year-old women whom we see around us have faces ranging from smooth to grooved, although almost all have some wrinkles. Wrinkles are an inevitable outcome of aging, but they can also be exacerbated by smoking, by exposure to ultra-violet rays, and by repeated facial expressions. Ruby, at 80, has an unlined face with only a few "crow's feet" around her eyes and the telltale upper lip lines of a former smoker. Some women much younger than Ruby have wrinkled faces from sun exposure. But by age 100, most old women will be wrinkled from face to legs—from head to toe. These wrinkled, sagging faces become, for women, the target of age-denying procedures, from the application of creams to Botox to repeated face-lifts.

The most common and least invasive modification of the old woman's face and skin is creams or lotions, used by (so far as we know) almost all the old women who talked with or wrote to us. Susan Bordo, who at age 56 expresses feminist "outrage" over media, marketing and body modifications, admits "Am I immune? Of course not. My bathroom shelves are littered with expensive age-defying lotions and potions" (2003: 3). Bordo points out that it is not only privileged women who attempt to make their faces more youthful; those who shop at Kmart buy much cheaper versions of these lotions and potions—which we suspect are all the same and do no good—but we use the expensive products anyway. And we wear makeup to smooth over our facial flaws.

As we saw in the last part, many of the old women wear mascara, eyeliner and eyeshadow to enhance their eyes. Makeup—foundation, powder and blusher—is also used to smooth and cover the skin of the face and minimize wrinkles. Although some women used makeup in their early teens or twenties, others adopted the practice as their faces aged.

Kathi: "I did not wear any makeup until I was in my thirties. I had long straight hair and I was sort of a hippie."

Carol: "I wore makeup from around thirteen." We both still apply the full mask: foundation, rouge, powder, eyebrow pencil, eyeshadow, eyeliner and mascara.

Old women's approaches to makeup vary from minimalist to maximalist. A minimalist approach is typified by Meredith, who says she uses "moisturizer only . . . I wear makeup for events, and sometimes if I am in the mood to bother." The maximalist approach is exemplified by Alice, who wears foundation and powder, blusher, false eyelashes and glossy lipstick. A few women alternate minimalist with maximalist. Annette says of another woman:

> "It is so odd. Sometimes we see her with makeup, looking normal. At other times she goes out with nothing—her eyes look bald, her skin has whitish patches and her mouth is sort of blue."

Consistency, for the old women's faces, is key; the mask of youthfulness cannot be dropped at will without the consequences of commentary.

Old (and young) women have used face creams and worn makeup since the Egyptians and ancient Greeks; in some historical eras, this was also true of men. The Roman poet Ovid, writing around the time of the birth of Christ, recommended the use of cosmetics to women because "Art improves nature . . . learn what method will your charms prolong." He suggests making a paste of poppies and water and applying it to the cheeks and provides an elaborate recipe for face powder (Piepenbring, 2014). The ancient ideal for a woman was a white face, kept from agricultural work in the sun. Face makeup has been a given for Western women since Greece and Rome, although fashions have moved from white faces to tanned and back. Whatever the color of the skin, it should appear smooth and unblemished; lips pink or red, glossy with lipstick; eyes framed in eyeshadow, liner and mascara. Unlike wealthy Roman women—who had slaves dedicated to applying their mistresses' cosmetics several times a day (Stewart, 2007)—we women generally apply our own, although there may be visits to a facialist, especially for the removal of facial hair. In the present day, the cosmetic industry serving young and old alike is a multi-billion-dollar, multi-national business.

Although, arguably, old faces need makeup more than young faces, makeup marketing in the glossy magazines features the young—the same is true, oddly, of hair dye. The internet is a bit more expansive, however, perhaps responding to the age of those who Google and email. The face of a model said to be 64 appears on Carol's laptop screen, with a smooth-skinned face and a long, dark-streaked mane of shiny silver hair. The woman points out that makeup should be tailored to the age of the face it intends to adorn. When Carol clicks on the ad—for an ad it is—it turns out that the model not only provides makeup tips ("no eye-shadow") but also sells her own line of cosmetics for the over-60 crowd.

Makeup can be quite expensive and represents enormous market-places. Carol wears the kind of makeup found at stores such as Target and Walmart: mascara is $11, foundation $13, and eyeliner $10—and that is just a start. For the expensive makeup found at stores such as Nordstrom and Bloomingdale—the ones that Kathi buys—those price tags would be in the over-$50 range. But very few of the well-enough-off old women refrain from wearing makeup, whatever the cost. Bella has white hair and wears mascara, face powder and red lipstick. She says of a 90-year-old friend:

> "She has her hair dyed black, it looks quite fake. She recently stopped wearing makeup. I said to her, 'You can't do that. Your face looks awful!'"

Women turn to professionals for the more invasive facial procedures. Attempts to make skin youthful again can involve scraping or burning it off, filling it out or pulling it up. Skin peels remove rough and wrinkled skin, to be replaced with a smoother regrowth. Botox and other toxins are inserted under the skin of the forehead, cheeks or lips to mimic the fuller curvatures of youth. Face-lifts, forehead lifts, and eye procedures rely on stretching the skin over a smaller area to decrease wrinkling. There are undoubtedly far more procedures than just listed, but that is enough for we old women at the moment. Body adornment and modi-fication are part of a consumer economy in which "Older people are moving from being publicly positioned as needy subjects . . . to active, powerful, and even greedy consumers" (Price and Livsey, 2015: 310).

A number of the old women have had face-lifts. LouAnn, 82, is a veteran of the knife. She says:

> I had my first plastic surgery in my forties. I was out in the sun
> so much that my skin was wrinkled and I looked like someone of

fifty-five. . . . I have had just about every part of my body lifted. . . . I don't like the way I look and I think I will have another facelift.

And a few months later, she did.

We saw LouAnn that afternoon; her mouth was swollen, bruised and lopsided. She said, before we could ask, "I had some work done, fat put into my face."

Carol: "From where?"
LouAnn: "From my thighs. They inject it."
Kathi: "Did it hurt?"
LouAnn: "No, I was asleep."

Nora, on her eightieth birthday, was complimented by one of our party: "Looking good!" Nora replied, "Well, if I don't look good I call my plastic surgeon." Between 80 and 82 she had several more facial procedures.

The old women speak of their own and others' facial procedures judgmentally. Women who have not had Botox or face-lifts (but could afford them) speak disapprovingly of those who have had them, comparing them to Joan Rivers or pointing out how they cannot smile or frown. Women who have had minor face-lifts speak disapprovingly of those who have had radical or multiple face- and body-lifts. Francie says:

"I have had reasonable work—well I think it is. My friend has had so much work. She has had her eyebrows lifted and you can see the scars. She has scars at her hairline. She has had every part of her body lifted."

Carol: "Her butt?'
Francie (laughing): "Well, not her butt, she doesn't need that lifted!"

As Eve comments, "Everything can be lifted."

For women such as Nora, Eve and LouAnn, old age does not put an end to their search for a slender body and a wrinkle-free face. We were discussing, with LouAnn, photographs of 100-year-old women that are posted (with their permission) on the internet. LouAnn said, firmly, "If I live to be a hundred, I'm going to be sucked and tucked as long as the money holds out." And money is certainly a consideration. Kathi's cousin's face-lift cost $60,000. A half-lifetime of face and body work can literally cost a fortune.

Feminists—especially when young—have been outspoken about the ideological inappropriateness of "having work done." But as they age, feminist professional women may begin to rethink their judgments. Debora Spar, president of Barnard College, is 53; she writes in "Aging and my Beauty Dilemma" (2016) that

> When it comes to aging . . . I am torn . . . like most women in my feminist-leaning, highly educated peer group . . . I am ideologically opposed to intervening in such a natural and inevitable process as simply getting on in years.
>
> (2016)

But Spar is, in her own words, "a two-faced hypocrite." She adds:

> Almost every woman I know colors her hair. . . . And . . . many . . . will quietly confess to a shot of Botox from time to time, or a dose of filler to soften their smiles.

Sheila Nevins, a Barnard graduate, describes herself as "betraying my liberal, earnest, sixties self" by having face-lifts (2017: 9). Rosie, a left-wing feminist, says

> "I will be 75 soon, and I am noticing horrid signs of aging: Crepey skin up and down my arms—legs, too; serious facial wrinkles, not to mention neck and throat. I have always scoffed at 'having work done' and am now considering it."

Under the face, as Rosie bemoans, are the chin and the neck. A double chin is one feature of excess weight, both in youth and in old age.

A scrawny neck is more likely among the thin elderly. Nora Ephron, in her book *I Feel Bad About My Neck*, says "I hate my neck . . . if you saw my neck, you might feel bad about it too." She details the horrors of old women's necks: chicken, turkey, gobbler, scrawny, fat, loose, crepey, banded, wrinkled, stringy, saggy, flabby and mottled—not to mention double chins (Ephron, 2006). Meredith, 75, picks "turkey" as her own neck descriptor and says, "Like Nora Ephron, I feel bad about my neck!" Then there is "the hangman's dilemma neck, like, when you have a neck that kind of goes from your chin to your chest" (Brooks, 2017: 53). Ephron pointed out that if an old woman wanted to have her neck surgically lifted, she has to also have her face lifted. Ellen told us (and many others) of her intention to have her face lifted just before she turned 70, mainly because of her flabby neck. Afterward, she spoke of how easy the procedure had been, and—at $10,000—how relatively inexpensive; a resident of Southern California, she had it done in Mexico.

Double chins and hangman's dilemma necks can be disguised by various forms of coverage; Nora Ephron says that she and her friends all wear turtleneck sweaters when they go out to lunch. Most of the time turtlenecks are not worn in Southern California, but turkey necks and double chins can be swathed in gauzy scarves. Indeed, almost any part of the public body can be concealed by being swathed in something—hats, scarves, gloves—but less so in warmer climes. Faces, chins, necks, hands and other parts of the body, unswathed, speak of age with wrinkles, age spots and other blemishes.

Atop our faces is our hair—the "crowning glory" of women's heads, thick and lush, framing our faces. Young hair is every shade from platinum to black. . . . By 70—and for some much earlier—hair has turned white or gray, dull of texture, and thinning. So—the old women, most of us, color our hair—something that both the privileged and the less privileged can afford. A study done in 2008—albeit by one of the dye manufacturers—found that 78% of all women dye their hair. So it is not just the old women whom we know, and ourselves, that use hair color.

Coloring hair is an individual decision, but it is situated within a web of cultural, gender, economic and relational expectations and issues. In our Western culture, non-gray or -white hair is associated with youth;

youth is prized over age—and one solution is to dye aging hair, which can be done in a salon or through the purchase of a kit. Look on any hair-color shelf in any drugstore, and you will see many boxes of color options, from light blond to black (and including gray!), most of them for women. The men's kits are labeled "for men only" and offer a narrower range of hues. It is clear men are expected to stay youthful, and women even more so. Hair coloring is one body modification affordable for all but the poorest old women; boxed kits can be found for as little as $2.99.

In addition to culture, economics and gender, relationships—husbands or partners, mothers, fathers and children—form a background chorus to a woman's decision to color her hair. A husband may prefer his wife not to have gray or white hair. A child may feel ashamed of her mother's age and white hair. A mother may be a role model for coloring hair or a counter-model for refusing to color it. Kathi grew up knowing that her mother, Peggy—who was a natural platinum blonde in her youth—later colored her gray hair blond. Kathi started coloring her own hair when gray began to appear, at first using salon colorists to apply streaks of blond. When the gray hairs became too numerous, she began dying her own hair to approximate her original light ash brown color.

Carol grew up knowing that most mothers had naturally blond or brown hair, and that some women who were becoming gray dyed their hair. Carol remembers that from at least the age of 7 she absolutely hated the way her mother, Mabs, looked. Older than most mothers, Mabs was gray haired and stout. By the time Carol was in high school, Mabs looked like the mother of her much younger husband, Ralph, and Carol, dressed up in the dumpy clothing, hats, and white gloves of the late 1950s, looked more like Ralph's wife than his daughter.

So when Carol started to see gray hairs on her own head in her early thirties, there was never any question about whether or not to cover the gray. The first step was frosting: instead of white streaks, Carol's brown hair had blond streaks. But the gray began to outpace the brown, and by her forties the solution was blond hair—which remains to this day. Carol's mother had warned her never to have long hair after she turned 25—today, Carol has long hair at the age of 74. Other mother-daughter dyads we have met repeated the oppositional hair dying/gray-hair dynamic that we have seen. Teresa refused to dye her hair as it went gray during her fifties, while her 80-year-old mother dyed her white hair brown and nagged Teresa continually about how she would look much better with dyed hair.

While the coloring of gray or white hair may be done to maintain a youthful sexual allure for a partner (or the hope for one), it can also be because of a small son or daughter. Rosie, pregnant at 40 with her second child, was mortified when a colleague at work told her that her gray hair made her look old. She says:

"I bought some hair dye and colored my hair right away. I continued to color it all the way through my son's childhood, elementary school, junior high school, high school, and college. I saw him all the way through."

Gloria Vanderbilt also describes starting to color her hair when, in her early forties, she gave birth to her son Anderson Cooper:

"I want to be young parents" [her husband said]. I immediately took the hint and started coloring my hair.
(Cooper and Vanderbilt, 2016: 184)

Hair coloring is a topic of debate among aging academic feminists. Some, like Germaine Greer, allow their hair to grow gray and their wrinkles to stay. Others partake somewhat of cosmetic "age denying." A photograph on the internet of Susan Bordo at 69 shows her with dark hair; Gloria Steinem's hair still looks fairly dark, with a white streak. Photographs of socialist-feminist Lynne Segal, born in 1944, show her with bright red hair. A comment on her *Feminist Times* article "Who's Afraid of Old Age?" reads, "From her photo I guess Lynne dyes her hair. Why?" (Segal, 2013). The "why" is obvious. Old women and men dye their because they want to appear younger than they are and they do not want gray or white hair. That women do so more frequently attests to the greater significance for women of a youthful-appearing, sexually appealing body.

At some point, later or sooner, women who dye their hair may either let it grow out or have the color stripped or gradually modified to white or gray. Later: we know several women who stopped coloring their hair in their mid-eighties. Sooner: some women in their forties to seventies stop coloring their hair for a number of reasons. Tamara, 62, stopped dying her hair in her forties because she and her husband were going around the world in a sailboat. Rosie stopped dying hers in her early seventies, saying that "I read a few articles on what the dye was doing to me and I did not like it"—plus her son was out of college. Lisa stopped dying hers because of "an extreme allergy."

Lisa, at 60, describes her experience with growing out her hair and what it means for body and self:

> Aging sucks. It requires a constant adaptation to a "new normal"—and adaptation is not my superpower! My husband and I have both experienced health issues in the last year, but the hardest ones for me have been those that strike at my appearance. I developed a significant allergy to hair dye and had to quit, cold turkey. All of the youth/beauty stuff that I've read and written about became painfully salient. It's one thing to critique the feminine beauty ideal philosophically—it's another thing to challenge it in day-to-day embodiment! I could write a book about the (hair) grow-out journey, but another woman already did so rather well—Anne Kreamer, "Going Grey." Fortunately, my hair is white so it sort of reads as platinum. And the curls might signal youth. But the comments I have gotten, almost all from women, have been so illuminating. Lots of "you are so BRAVE" and often, "I wish I could go natural but my husband won't let me." Yikes. Luckily my husband has been completely supportive—in fact, he loves it. Probably for some weird psychological reason, but I'm just going to appreciate it.

Lisa's white hair, like our bodies, was not—for a while—herself. After a year she still had not posted a photograph of herself with white hair on Facebook; she smiled out at the world with dark curls. Two years later, however, she was on FB with white hair.

Rosie, Lisa and Tamara all invoke the greater "naturalness" of gray or white over dyed hair. A recent book, *Going Grey*, makes the same point, valorizing authenticity over attempting to look more youthful—and mocking the latter in ways we saw in the introductory chapter. Anne Kreamer (2007) who had dyed her hair various colors since her late twenties and was then 49, saw a photograph of herself with her hair dyed dark brown

> All my years of careful artifice, attempting to preserve what I thought of as a youthful look, was ripped away. . . . I was pretending to be someone I wasn't. Someone still young.
>
> (p. 5)

Tellingly subtitled *What I Learned About Beauty, Sex, Work, Motherhood and Everything Else That Really Matters*, Kreamer's book is a paean to the authenticity and naturalness of undyed gray or white hair. She exhorts old women to "Get Real!" (p. 49).

Kreamer (2007) stopped coloring her dyed hair because she suddenly saw it, in a photograph, as a "flat, dark helmet." The dark helmet and her subsequent turn to gray are illustrated by the "before" and "after" photograph on the jacket of her book. Kathi: 'She looks about twenty years older in the 'after' photograph." Carol: "She looks fifteen years older in the 'after' photograph." Her hair does not look gray in the "after" photograph, it looks brownish with a white streak. The cover of the book features a beautiful head of silvery hair, streaked with light, shiny and thick, that actually looks professionally colored. Carol: "if I had to pick how my hair looked from *Going Grey*—the cover, the before, or the after, I would pick the cover." And now we discover that gray hair is not just for the older set. At the time of writing this book on old bodies, there appears to be a cultural turn toward "silver" hair for younger people— bright silver for the young, dull gray for the old. The March 2016 issue of the glamor magazine *Allure* has three photographs of women with silver hair who appear to be in their twenties.

Some women, such as Lisa, are forced to stop coloring their hair and do not like it. Others, such as Kreamer, want to feel authentic. Clarissa's hairdresser is gradually altering her hair from a dyed blond to white. Clarisa says, "I will be seventy-six next year. When is it time to stop pretending?" Fawn, 62, who dresses quite plainly and goes without makeup, still colors her hair: "I am not quite ready." Some non-colorers say that they like their natural white, gray or other color. Anne, 74, colored her hair for years but stopped when she was 64. The hair that grew out was "a natural, youthful strawberry blond!" Bella dyed her hair for about six months when she was in her sixties but got tired of the cost and time of salon procedures. She likes her white hair with a touch of gray because "it goes with my favorite colors: blue, brown and purple."

The point of dying hair is to make it look "natural" despite the "unnaturalness" of the process. This means that the hair should not only be blond, brown or red, it should also be thick, shiny and with shades of difference within the tones (unlike Kreamer's "dark helmet," which does seem unusual given the amount of money she says she spent coloring it). Debora Spar's comment about facial and bodily interventions is equally true of hair: "the bar of normal keeps going up." A few decades ago hair was dyed to cover the gray, and roots were dispatched. But today old hair has to match youthful hair as closely as possible, meaning that it is dyed not one color but two, three or four. Laura compares her own hair with her sister's; they are both in their early sixties:

> "My sister does her own hair, which means it is one shade of brown. It costs her about ten dollars. Mine was looking too blond, so I had it lowlighted. It costs around $100 for the cut and the tip."

The $100—or $400—dark salon coloring job has to be repeated month after month, week after week in order to avoid the showing of gray or white roots—to show roots invalidates the whole façade of naturalness. Dark dyed hair that shows roots is not uncommon as we go around the shops and streets outside our community, but it is unusual, and comment-worthy, within our group. "Why doesn't she do something about her hair" is a common critique of white showing at the roots of dark hair.

On the other hand, blond hair with brown roots is youth-affirming. We remember the fifties and sixties, when a brunette who dyed her hair blond was required to police those dark roots and have none showing—pretending to be a natural blonde. By contrast, young news-casters and weather reporters in the mid-2000s often sport blond hair with lots of dark roots showing. Some of the old women have adopted this look, with their white or gray hair dyed dark at the roots and blond at the tips, a variant on the two-color "frosted" hair common in the 1980s and 1990s.

Hair dying has an effect not only on the color but on the texture of hair. Gray hair tends to be coarser and dryer than whatever color it devolved from, so that it lacks shine and bounce. Candy complains that "My hairdresser gets a good color, but the texture isn't good, my hair is dry and flat." When first dyed, hair is thicker and shinier than the gray it covers. But the longer the old woman goes between coloring, the less her hair will shine and bounce. The shorter the time between coloring, the more permanent damage to whatever hair she has left. Catch-22. So, some old women return to their gray or white hair. By their mid-80s, most of the old women have accepted gray or white hair.

As they age, women's hair strands get thinner and fewer, with per-haps a bald spot at the crown; these natural processes are exacerbated by dying hair. Women with thinning hair turn to a variety of products, from spray-on color with bits of fake hair in it to lotions that promise to grow new hair. Marlene, at 70, has beautifully coiffed blond hair that she says is so thin she uses a topically-applied hair growth product daily. Bald spots are sometimes seen among women at the tops of our heads, but mostly we grow front hair to cover them, or use spray on products or wear hats before our next coloring session. Spouses and partners are enlisted to make sure the telltale markers of an aging head are (at least temporarily) covered.

Hair is indeed a woman's crowning glory in this culture, making bald-ness or severely thinning hair serious problems for women. Baldness may be due to hereditary factors or medical treatments, especially those for cancer. Although there are examples of some young women who shave their heads to look interesting, stylish or different, old women who are bald, regardless of the reason, often choose to wear head scarves, caps or wigs as cover. Alice says that her hair fell out when her third husband died suddenly, and she has worn wigs ever since—short, curly, smooth, red and blond. The wigs are expensive and may be somewhat "natural" looking, but they are obviously wigs and thereby constitute artifice as such rather than the artfulness of imitating youth. On the other hand, a gray wig is not so telltale. Mandy routinely wore a gray wig after her medication made her hair fall out. Few were aware of this until she appeared one day with about 2 inches of white and gray hair that looked like a crew-cut. She said, "It is too hot to wear a wig." The compliments flew—"You look great"; "Wonderful haircut"; "Way to go." The opposite scenario occurred when Joanna started wearing wigs; her hair had been thinning for several years. For her, the typical responses from friends and acquaintances were: "You look great!" "Love the hair."

And then there are the various facial hair sites: eyebrows, eyelashes, eyebrows and—alas—chins and upper lips. Men have beards and mustaches; women do not—until they begin to get old. The hair that disappears from legs, arms, underarms and pubis reappears on the upper lip and chin of old women (de Beauvoir, 1972: 26). Women of ancient Rome removed facial hair with arsenic (Stewart, 2016); our methods are not so drastic, but we still don't want facial hair. Today, there are several methods other than arsenic for removing facial hair including twee-zers, threading, waxing, electrolysis, laser treatment, depilatory cream and shaving. When she was in her teens, Kathi watched her mother methodically pluck hairs, with a tweezer, from around her lips and chin. At the time the action had no relevance; aging had no relevance. When we were both in our forties, Carol—apparently; she does not remember—requested tweezers to remove a hair from Kathi's chin.

In her fifties, Kathi watched a woman in her seventies having her face waxed at the salon they both frequented. So she tried the same process, but this caused clogged pores. Later she turned to electrolysis to remove pesky hairs from her upper lip and chin, but found the procedure time-consuming, expensive and not very effective. She was told that it sometimes required multiple treatments to destroy the follicles, so the tweezers went back into action. One consequence of Kathi's cousin's face-lift (besides needing follow-up face-lifts) was that she grew a wiry stubble on her face and chin. Her solution was to shave her face with some regularity. Indeed, shaving is a last resort for those old women whose facial hair begins to outpace their tweezers.

Eyelids and eyebrows combine to cause medical and cosmetic difficulties for old men and women. Some eyelid lifting is considered medical—and reimbursed—because the drooping interferes with vision. Other procedures are cosmetic. Eve says: "When I did my last facial procedure, they pumped some fat into my eyebrows as well as my cheeks." Not identifying with old people, Eve adds: "Old people's skin around their eyebrows get so thin that they look skeletal." Aging men often have bushy, wild eyebrows; while some women's eyebrows become thin, others manage to be thin and bushy at the same time. Women attempt to reduce the bushiness with tweezers or scissors in an attempt to not look like old men, and then attempt to smooth the color out with hair dye or eyebrow pencil. As of this writing, eyebrows seem to be at the mercy of extensive scrutiny and repair, a significant aspect of beauty marketing. There are advertisements for "threading" eyebrows to make them shapelier; Nora Ephron (2006) had this done while she was in her fifties. Although the quest for eyebrow perfection (as opposed to stopgap repair) seems to belong mostly to young women—and men—old women may also take a new interest in their eyebrows:

Bertha, 74: "I have found my eyebrows again—at least I have had them
found for me. They disappeared a while ago, and now they are back."
She wiggles her forehead, and, indeed, we see eyebrows. "My friend
is a cosmetologist and she did it for me."

Eyebrows can also be restored by tattooing. Inge, when she was in her late sixties, had eyebrows tattooed above her eyes when her eyebrow hairs disappeared. She said she did it because her husband "is always telling me to hurry and get ready for something, so I got my eyebrows done." In addition to her eyebrow tattoos, had eyeliner tattooed on each eyelid above her eyelashes, and her lips tattooed pink-red so that she would be able to rush out without bothering with eyebrow pencil, eyeliner or lipstick.

Most of the women use eyebrow pencil to restore their eyebrows' shape and color, eyeliner to define their eyes and mascara to thicken and darken their eyelashes. Some wear eyeshadow to pick up the color of their eyes or clothing, despite the 64-year-old makeup entrepreneur's admonition not to wear eyeshadow because it accents wrinkled eyelids. A couple of the old women wear false eyelashes, something that was a lot more common a few decades ago.

The "improvement" of women's face, hair and other parts of the body exemplify what Hurd (2010: 3) calls "the relentless 'mining' of the female body for potential 'flaws' in need of beauty intervention . . . [with] more and more beauty products." We have seen that the mandate for these "improvements" is deeply embedded in Western culture. The tenacity of the cosmetic shaping of women's bodies over centuries is one factor in the failure of feminist pleas for natural aging to be taken up (outside their own circles). The other factor is the marketplace. Selling and advertising has greatly expanded, as Hurd says, the arenas and technologies of improvement, from hair dyed one color to hair dyed five colors; from eyebrow pencil to eyebrow salons; from douches to Brazilian waxes and labiaplasties.

Although cosmetic body modifications can be done at home, some women prefer to go to a hair, nail or eyebrow salon. There is some evidence that salons function for women as gendered homes away from family homes, where stories and life events can be told and shared. For older women—customers and workers—they provide "a place of mutual care and support," where the bodily effects of aging are modified in accordance with cultural and ageist notions of proper bodies. But these salons are also a space in which "older women's lives and identities are validated and recognized against a backdrop of broader patterns of social exclusion and ageism" (Ward, 2015: 143).

So far as we know, there are no salons for the removal of nose hair; this is a do-it-yourself job. The hair inside the nose is functionally useful in trapping bits and pieces, but cosmetically unsightly if visible. Lily, who at 70 found her nose hair growing almost to the point of visibility, took steps to reduce its length and volume:

"At first I clipped that nose hair, but one time I clipped the inside of my nose. So then I tweezed the nose hair. I got an infection from that (sighs and laughter) so now I just leave it alone."

The nose itself may present problems as we age, both cosmetic and medical. The cartilage of the nose droops with age, causing a nose-tip falling that makes the nose look larger. Cosmetic surgeons do several types of rhinoplasty, one of which involves the lifting of the aging nose.

Under the nose is the ever-smiling mouth, with its tongue and teeth. Americans are regarded by Europeans and Russians as smiling too much and thus creating wrinkles—of course those Europeans and Russians may have wrinkled upper lips from smoking. Tongues do not seem to vary much over the decades, while mouths are a bit more problematic. We may mimic youth with lip liner and glossy lipstick. Some old (and not so old) women have these upper lip lines "filled" with various substances and/or have their lips made puffy. Cosmetic dermatology is big business among the privileged. And inside those lips are our teeth. Nikki is 30 years old; she is laughing, all her teeth visible as she throws her head back. Every tooth in her head is white—on the outside, on the inside. Kathi and Carol have whitened teeth. But if we threw our heads back and laughed, the bottoms of our teeth would be more colorful—some white, some gray, some gold.

In the youthful—and now everyone's—ideal, visible teeth are white and straight and there should be thirty-two (plus four wisdom teeth). Medical and routine tooth care are recommended, throughout life, to maintain tooth health: brushing, flossing, water picking, and tartar removal. There can be problem teeth at any age, but in old age teeth may cause trouble at an increasing rate. By old age, there may be no teeth or rotted teeth. Horace says of some poor old woman of antiquity: "Your teeth are black. Antiquity ploughs furrows in your ancient forehead . . . your breasts are as flaccid as the dugs of a mare" (de Beauvoir, 1972: 122). Among twentieth-century women with resources for dentistry, this is not going to happen—at least the black teeth part of it.

We are supposed to retain and attend to our thirty-two teeth in the cosmetic ways (often expensive) that foster a properly smiling mouth: retaining them with bridges, replacing them with implants, straightening them (hopefully done at an earlier age), capping, and tooth whitening. False teeth are not allowed. We are all very aware of how our teeth are supposed to look:

> Carol is talking with 80-year-old Frances about height. "There are so many tall women around here that I am always looking at teeth, necklaces or tits." Frances's hand flies to her mouth; her teeth are straight and white enough to look natural. "I am due for a tooth whitening soon," she says self-consciously. "Your teeth look fine," Carol says.

Gloria Steinem endorses—complete with celebrity photo—a tooth whitening system called Supersmile that she says she uses to maintain "healthy" teeth.

As it is with cosmetic facial and body procedures and with hair, the bar is constantly being raised on teeth. It might once have sufficed to have all one's teeth and not false teeth, and those teeth could be various shades of white or cream, as long as they did not move into the territory of brown or gray. Now, teeth must be straight rather than crooked, and a brilliant white that sometimes resemble the false teeth of old. Cosmetic dentistry is the beneficiary of this bar-raising, with rising costs to go along. Both Kathi and Carol have had their teeth whitened. Kathi's dentist wanted to put "invisible" braces on her lower teeth to straighten them, despite the fact that given the way she smiles those teeth are rarely seen. She declined.

Old women whose smiles violate the norms of the teeth are observed and commented upon. Sylvia, when she was in her mid-sixties, sometimes appeared to have all her teeth, but at other times her back teeth were missing—which made clear that they were false. Sylvia often began a conversation during a social occasion with her back teeth in, then reached into her mouth and slipped them into her purse. Because of Sylvia's violation of local appearance norms she was widely known as looking "like a bag lady." Annette says:

"I saw Sylvia the other day at the grocery store. She looked like a bag lady. She had no teeth. Her hair was hanging down all grown out gray. She was very thin and had on these raggedy clothes."

The loss of teeth is a *memento mori* for the old women, and they will (if they can) pay for expensive dental procedures. At 70, Carol had an upper right tooth that had to be removed. As she told Kathi, "Nothing that has happened to me yet has made me feel as old as not having that tooth." It was expensive to have the tooth removed, but it would have been more expensive, and even more painful, to have the tooth replaced by an implant, so Carol did not do it. Other women have had tooth implants and bridges to avoid losing teeth.

Various aspects of teeth and dentistry are affected by aging as well as by the use of drugs. Teeth falling out from the use of crystal meth—"meth mouth"—is not something we have run across among the old women. But smokers' tooth loss has occurred. Sylvia and SueAnn—both of them well-off financially—lost teeth because of having smoked and continuing to smoke; as we saw, Sylvia let her teeth fall out, while SueAnn had them painfully replaced by implants. Women and men who have had their teeth straightened by various cosmetic dental methods may find that their teeth, diverted from their "natural" situation, may move and fall out later in life.

There is much more to the head than its teeth, hair and face, as we saw in the last chapter. But this is enough for now; let us move down the public body to the places where hair may be observed in public—the underarms, legs, and arms. Although our underarms may rarely be on display as we get older, they can appear if we wear a swimsuit or play tennis with a sleeveless shirt. Underarm shaving in America is said to date from May 1915, when the magazine *Harper's Bazaar* published a picture of a woman in a sleeveless dress—both of these revolutionary concepts. Ironically, while young women today often shave their pubic hair, there is simultaneously a trend to grow—and even dye—underarm hair.

The ancient Egyptians shaved their bodies from head to toe, including pubic and head hair and eyebrows, with pumice stones or bronze razors. We modern Americans pick and choose which parts we will shave or wax. As we saw in Part I, the growing or removal of pubic hair varies with culture and over time. While it is common in the here and now to shave the legs of the public female body, it is less common to shave her hairy arms. The shaving of legs became popular in a postwar era of sheer nylon stockings and has continued into our era of bare-legged sports. We old women continue to shave our underarms and legs, even though, in the words of so many of us, "We do not have any hair."

With or without hair, our arms and legs, although sometimes covered, are at other times part of the public body. We saw in Chapter 2 how the upper arms failed first, with softening muscles and crepey, hanging skin. By 60, many women no longer wear sleeveless or cap-sleeved top; the arms must be covered to the elbow. Softening muscles and a cottage-cheese-like texture is common in old thighs; athletic or walking women move from tennis dresses to Bermuda shorts or knee-length skorts. The lower arms begin to develop their own droops and wrinkles—and by 80, both arms and legs are wrinkled. Eve wears clothing from her wrists to her ankles, showing off a tall and slender body in outline, concealing the flaws of age.

Every decade throughout history has had prescriptions and proscriptions about what female body parts should be made public and which ones should remain private. While underarms were first shown to the American public in 1915, navels remained hidden until the 1950s, when the first bikinis were seen on beaches in the South of France. During the early 2000s fashion trends for the young included low-slung jeans, pierced navels, and see-through tops. In a private club, a 70-year-old woman who showed off her thong panties and skimpy bra through a white gauze dress generated many tsks, rolled eyes, and comments among the other old women.

Much more frequently observed than our underwear are our hands and—in warm Southern California—our feet. Our hands change as we age, and generally not for the better—although at 70, there are good hands and bad hands in the owners' eyes. The good hands are youthful, with clear skin, straight, unbent fingers, and nails that are either also good, or have been covered with polish. The bad hands show their age, with wrinkles, age spots, and fingers that point in various directions because the joints are out of joint. These descriptions fit Kathi's hands and Carol's, respectively.

Good hands may be given elaborate manicures and function (hopefully) to draw attention away from other aspects or parts of the body. Ellie, 70, weighs perhaps 400 pounds. She has beautiful hands: slender and without age spots. She maintains her nails carved into perfect long ovals in a bright lacquered red, with monthly visits to a salon for acrylic maintenance and nail polishing. As we converse, Ellie waves her hands in the air to emphasize points. This tactic (as we think it is) is premised upon the youthfulness and normalcy of one pair of body parts, in contrast to the unbearable weight.

Bad hands have numerous issues, including medical problems such as arthritis. But bad hands do not stop there. The bones of our hands seem to send out shoots in search of something; our fingers bend when they were once straight. Our fingernails get ridges, somehow managing to become thinner and thicker at the same time. With their wrinkles and age spots, hands are the second most common target of what feminist writers call "Age Defying" procedures (Segal, 2013). The marketplace is ready to help with various bleaching creams for age spots, many of which have been around for decades. But until fairly recently age spots could not be removed by dermatologists, so that a face-lift might proclaim an old woman "65" while her hands proclaimed "80." Maggy had the age spots on her hands removed by laser when she was 65, saying:

> "I don't look in the mirror at my face all the time. But I do look at my hands. And they scream 'Old, old, old.'"

The functionality of hands as well as their appearance may change over time. Arthritis both gnarls and cripples fingers, making it difficult to hold objects or put on gloves. Hands lose strength; we may grip a hairbrush without pain, but we cannot hold on to it, and it drops to the floor. Jars are difficult to open, and locks resist our attempts to close or open them. For women whose hands were important to their adult selves—musicians, surgeons—losing the functionality of those hands means losing part of themselves. Kathi plays the piano and ukulele almost daily to keep her fingers limber; although she has never played professionally, her musicality is part of her identity. And so is her athleticism—which depends upon the feet as well as the body.

The feet—and the soles—the bottom of the public body. For the old women, feet can have various cosmetic and functional issues. *Our Bodies Ourselves* critiqued the cultural expectation that young women should wear high heels, the purpose of which is to make the woman taller and throw off the alignment of her legs and body to look "sexier." It is clear that many decades later young women have not thrown aside their high heels; indeed, they are higher than ever. Some of the old women wear high heels on some occasions, mainly at formal events. But otherwise they wear shoes that enable them to walk without fear of falling or cramping.

While young women generally have "normal" feet free of functional afflictions, not so the old women. As we age, our feet develop many ways of tormenting us both functionally and cosmetically. Carol has had surgeries on her bunions and hammertoes several decades ago, when it had become difficult to drive a car without pain. Various conditions can make it difficult for feet to propel the body in motion, from diabetes to tendonitis. Karyn, 75: "I have times when I cannot walk because of my foot pain. I have plantar fasciitis and some kind of little nodules that hit the nerves."

Karyn has slender feet with straight toes; they may hurt, but they look attractive in sandals, and they can fit into closed-toe shoes. Not so many of the old feet of the old women. Kathi and Carol sit on the seawall, legs dangling toward the sand, both wearing flip-flops.

> Kathi's feet are slender and well-shaped, with small, straight toes. The skin of her feet is tanned, smooth and hairless. Her toenails are well shaped, painted a coral color. Carol's feet are wide and long, with short, unpainted toenails (not rough or yellowed, yet). Her feet are asymmetrical. On her left foot, two of the toes are still hammered, and face each other, with the remaining toes veering right or left.

We look down at our feet in those pretty rhinestone-encrusted flip-flops, and the contrast between the footwear and the feet underlines the contrast between youth and age. Clarice and Carol compare feet:

We are looking down at our feet in flip-flops. Clarice's are slender and tanned, Carol's not so much.

Carol: "That scar—did you get bunion surgery?"
Clarice: "Yes, both sides, both feet. They hurt so much I could not wear shoes."
Carol: "I couldn't either—but I still can't!"
Clarice: "I can't either, I always wear these!"
Carol: "Me too!" We both laugh.

As people age, their fingernails and toenails thicken. Nail cells pile up as the nails' growth rate decreases. Fingernails' growth rate is less slow than toenails', and fingernails get more cosmetic attention, so they thicken less. But neither fingers nor toes are the dainty shell-like appendages of childhood and youth. Fingernails develop ridges, and toenails yellow and crack. Both can harbor infections and fungi. Sylvia caught us looking at her toenails, which were long, thick and yellow. She said, "Yes I know, I hate cutting my toenails, so I am turning into Howard Hughes." On another occasion, she had a yellow big toenail about two inches high sticking out of her sandal. Once more she caught us looking, and said, "It's a fungus, and I have got to go and have it taken care of, but I haven't found the time." A few months later:

Carol, looking at Sylvia's foot: "I see you had that toenail fungus taken care of."
Sylvia: "No, it just fell off by itself."

For those old people who don't want to or cannot cut their finger or toenails, there are salons that give manicures and pedicures, often including hand or foot massages. We were at a salon where:

> There is a very old woman sitting in one of the chairs, her feet in a foot bath. She has long gray hair, and her arms, bare to the elbow, are wrinkled and mottled. Her head droops while the "nail

woman" cuts and files her fingernails. By the time the procedure is finished, the old woman is asleep.

We did not see the old woman have her finger- or toenails painted, but many old women disguise the condition of their nails with polish or with products that strengthen and lengthen nails. These products and processes, though, have their dangers:

We are on a boat trip. Clarice has a large bandage on one finger.

Kathi: "What happened?"
Clarice: "I got my nails done and I got an infection under this nail." She pulls off the bandage to reveal an index fingernail that is lifted-up and oozing yellow pus. "I am not going to do this again."

Two months later we are on another boat trip. Clarice is wearing acrylic nails in the French style. We look at them; she says, "Yes, I did it again" (laughter).

Salon procedures for coloring and shaping nails constitute a sizable industry, together with thousands—millions?—of products that can be applied at home. Whatever color you want your finger- and toenails, just like whatever color you want your hair, it is there for you.

We show ourselves as public bodies from head to toe, adorned with enough coverage to show only what we wish in the way we wish. We are not likely to avail ourselves of burkas, so our faces and hair are almost always on view—and get the most attention, from us in the mirror and from others as the audience. Unless we are skiing or ice skating, we show our hands, feet, fingernails and toenails, all with cosmetic problems and remedial possibilities. To show our arms and legs is optional; however hot it is, we can always cover them if we wish. Together with our tall-or-short, fat-or-thin body in outline, we present ourselves to each other, and to the world, as old women. And we carry on, living our lives, loving whom we love, inside and despite our bodies.

5

THE BODY IN OUTLINE

Unbearable Weight

Weight and height are the scaffolding of the body in public and in private. Both are important for women and for men; in some ways height is more significant to men than women, and weight to women than men, although there are reversals. Height is important to women in old age, one bulwark against invisibility. Completing the body in outline are the shape and size of the breasts, belly and buttocks. Both men and women are supposed to have shapely buttocks and no bellies; only women's bodies should grow breasts. The body in outline is, in our Western culture, typically a covered body, clothed in its substantial parts; yet, some activities and some fashions involve the old women in revealing body segments.

Above all, for women, there is unbearable weight. In Western culture, slenderness embodies youth, and to be overweight is to feel the world's unbearable gaze upon us. Boys and young men are feminized by weight, with the breasts and belly of fertile women. Fat girls and young women are prematurely aged, with the breasts, bellies, double chins and facial hair growth of old women. Bordo (2003) has shown how the mass media reflect standards of slenderness that are unattainable for many young women, who, when they feel their weight as unbearable, may enter the anteroom of despair. Binge eating, purging, dieting, bulimia and anorexia are among the consequences.

The cultural demand for slenderness does not diminish with the decades. Older women, as the young, experience weight as unbearable.

As Clark and Bennett (2015: 135) note, "older women frequently indicate that their weight is central to their perception of body dissatisfaction." The culture and economy of slenderness is all around us. We gaze upon slender bodies in magazines and the mass media, where even those very few old women we see on the pages are thin. When women are old, not only our weight but our entire bodies become unbearable, year by year, piece by piece. As we saw in the previous chapter, the outlines of those bodies—together with heads, faces, hands and feet—are visible to the world as we go about our lives, on beaches, in locker rooms, in shops, at restaurants and bars. Bathing suits and bikinis are the minimal public coverage (unless one is a nudist), concealing private parts but revealing the body's height, weight and breast, belly and buttock shape and size

Height is an important aspect of the body in young adulthood—to be tall is proper for a man, not too short or tall is right for a woman. It is well known that short men suffer in comparison to tall men in arenas from self-esteem, to dating, to the workplace. Women are not expected to be tall, although they are also not expected to be shorter than about 60 inches. Several old women who were tall in their teens report that they had, then, wanted to be short. Eve says:

> "I was as tall as I am now at twelve, and I absolutely hated it. My mother said that I would like it later, but I did not believe her. But I did believe her when she told me to stand up straight, not hunch over to hide my height, and I am glad I did."

Now, at about 5-foot-10, Eve is tall, striking and slender.

Women who wear high heels may want to look sexy; they may also want to look taller, underlining the importance, for women as well as men, of not being short. Wednesday Martin (2015) describes upper-middle class Park Avenue women as exhibiting dominance through height accentuated by high heels. Women often lose inches as they grow older, but the relative height difference remains, and short old women are teased by taller ones. We were talking to Doris, 75, who was with six other women at a table:

"We noticed that a man who was about to speak at a podium had a shirt that had a stain on it and it was untucked. I was told to go and talk to him about it because I am the shortest one."

Old people often shrink over time, sometimes by as much as six inches, and sometimes to child size. To remain tall is to retain some grip on a former self, one who is adult and not child-like or elder-like.

Adding height is impossible without surgical intervention, although an illusion of extra inches can be obtained by various kinds of shoes and shoe inserts. But weight is, at least in theory, changeable—which makes being fat, or not losing weight, a cultural—and even moral—issue. There are fat old women, thin old women and old women who are of normal, slender—not comment-worthy—weight (size 6, 8, or 10 for a 5-foot-6 woman). Old women who are fat may always have been fat, or they may have been of normal weight when young. But if the body is larger than normal, the weight is unbearable. Our culture tells us so, reflecting our unworthiness back to us if we are fat. Cultural stigma, personal shame.

Kathi exemplifies the size 8 old woman, "watching" her weight successfully and complimented rather than criticized for her appearance/ body. Her weight has ranged from normal to thin throughout her life course, except for a few years when she developed Hashimoto's disease and lost her thyroid. Carol's weight has yo-yo'ed from normal to thin to fat, and she is currently fat. The ideal slender body is "natural" for many young women but takes a lot of effort for old women. Susan, 70, is an old woman who embodies the ideal.

Susan comes into the bar, looking, as usual, about 45 and looking, as usual, smiling and happy. She is of medium height and slender. Her hair is a light, streaked brown, long enough to almost reach her shoulders but short enough to show off silver and turquoise earrings. She has white teeth, arched eyebrows, long dark lashes (no false ones) and coral lips. Her tight jeans and boots high-light her legs and taut buttocks. She is wearing a fringed jacket with long sleeves. Her turtleneck sweater shows off high, firm, medium-sized breasts.

A lot of work has gone into Susan's embodiment, from "natural" diet and exercise to "unnatural" hair coloring, padding, makeup, teeth straightening and whitening, and at least one face-lift. She is also very beautiful.

Slender is the ideal body; thin/anorexic is seen as problematic, although not so much as fat:

> Belinda, her platinum blond hair in a chignon, is wearing a black sweater and palazzo pants. "Look at that . . . she is much too thin" says Viola. "I wonder if she is anorexic?" says someone—pretty much out of Belinda's hearing, but not necessarily.

In the general population of old women, self-starvation takes a form particular to the old, precipitated by dementia/forgetfulness, depression, lack of mobility and pain. But there are some old women whose anorexia takes the same pathway as the teenager girl's: a desire to lose weight, dieting and an iron control that takes over the self (Faulkner-Wiley, 2001; Bordo, 2003).

Old women diagnosed with depression or anorexia may be treated with electroconvulsive therapy (shock therapy). This treatment, like pharmaceuticals or surgery, involves the body and brain of the patient. A convulsion is induced using an electrical current (an earlier variation used insulin shock). Other brain-altering treatments for depressed or anxious people include the use of electromagnetic and magnetic devices to alter pathways in the brain. Convulsive treatment seems to have an "oppositional" effect: the catatonic are rendered more talkative and the combative more calm (Kneeland and Warren, 2009).

Wherever records of ECT are kept—and they are spotty in the United States—they show that in this and other English-speaking countries, the treatment's most common recipients are women aged 65 and older. The growing use of this treatment on old people has been noted since the 1980s (Kneeland and Warren, 2009) and has expanded to include some of the oldest old, with one woman reporting yearly treatment at age 100. There are psychiatric and other explanations for this demographic. Among the other explanations are old people becoming difficult for their caregiver to manage; lack of effectiveness, over time, of psychoactive drugs; and different insurance "pots" for different treatments.

The term "eating disorders" encompasses the purging as well as the fasting, the fat as well as the thin. Yo-yo dieting is common among the old women—and a few of the old men—who don't want to gain five pounds a year. Other couples and singles are defiantly stout but were slender in earlier decades. Their younger selves are displayed in wedding photos on tables or walls, I point at a photograph of a smiling young woman and ask Louise, "Who is that?" "That was me," she replied, "in one of my thin phases." For other couples, the saying "Jack Sprat could eat no fat, his wife could eat no lean" is descriptive, although it is usually the other way around. Georgina is about 50, tall and slender; her husband Josh is 70, stout, and short.

The combination of fat and short is commonplace among old women as well as some old men. Annette comments on what she calls "a nation of frogs":

> "We were walking around Disneyland last week. I saw a busload of old women walking around. They all sort of looked like me— short, fat, with short hair, and bent over. If they were all wearing green they would look like a nation of frogs."

Such observations align with the cultural realization that we are a nation of ageists. Ageism, like racism or sexism, takes the body and turns it into not just a physical but a moral category, and not in a good way (Calasanti and King, 2015; Gullette, 2015). But unlike the embodiments of race and sex, age will come to us all eventually, unless we die before 60. Age is stigmatizing; more so if it combined with fat.

Fat is stigmatizing, and it is shameful: in Jack LaLanne's words, when he was 95, "FAT. 'F' 'A' 'T.' Fatal. Awful Terrible." Face shaming, body shaming and fat shaming are common on the internet. A recent remake of the movie *Ghostbusters* stars women instead of men as the ghost-hunting heroes. One of them is Leslie Jones, a sturdy black woman. One of the mildest internet attacks on her by Milo Yiannopolous, a conservative internet troll, is: "Who You Gonna Call? Weightwatchers!"

Racist addenda to his body shaming attacks include referring to her as an ape (www.fusion.net). (To be fair, she did tweet Milo that he was a "faggot" who should be "gassed.") That there are far fewer trolls pursuing old than young women is not because old women are immune, it is that there are far fewer of them in the public eye. But there are some who dare appear before its gaze, from gray-haired academics to plump movie stars.

Aside from the preferences of Fat Admirers and Chubby Chasers, there is nothing good about fat in Western culture. As Bordo (2003) has pointed out, fat symbolizes appetite, greed, lack of self-control and the female body as opposed to the male mind or spirit. If there is anything good to be said about old age, it is that mind and spirit—men—can become more refined, educated and wise as time passes. But that is the male part of the mind-body dualism. The old fat woman is simply flesh; simply gross. So much so that two recently bereaved and grieving widows have said to us: "At least I will be losing weight."

But fat or thin, the public body adapts to its type through adornment. Slender women can wear a variety of clothing, although as they age they may decide to cover body parts that are no longer youthful: long or at least elbow length sleeves, dresses and pants that cover the knees or (preferably) go down to the ankle. Women who might be seen as anorexic may show off their bodies or they may hide their size and shape under layers of loose clothing. An old woman who walks in our neighborhood—apparently for most of the day—wears brightly colored clothes that hang over and cover her body. Over the past decade her gait has slowed—she limps a bit and lists to one side—but she continues to walk and walk.

Fat bodies adorn themselves in the full knowledge that they are not going to pull anything off. Black is the color of choice, with dark navy, brown, or purple close seconds. Wardrobe items are carefully chosen in the hope that they will minimize, or at least not maximize, the appearance of a fat body. Otherwise the audience observes and comments.

Carol: I go into the ladies' room. Joanna is examining herself in the long mirror. She is wearing jeans closely-fitted to her buttocks and thighs and a short blouse. She says, "Not quite right, what do you think?" I say, "A longer blouse?" We both laugh.

If you are fat, your tops should be loose and your bulges should be covered—if they are not, you will be noticed and sanctioned for your poor choice of clothing as well as for the unbearable weight itself.

An old body, slender or fat, concerns itself with adornment and dress. Slim old women may "continue to wear their jeans and pursue youthful, fashionable styles" (Twigg, 2015: 151), although they may eschew styles that reveal drooping body parts. Fat old women have less to choose from, and they may make different clothing choices from their thin compatriots. We learn that batwing sleeves cover not only the wrinkles but the fat of an upper arm and, like Joanna, that a longer top conceals a bulge at the waist. And our jeans are probably elasticized.

People generally do not comment on yellowed teeth or graying hair, but they do pay attention to weight. "You've lost weight!" is a not infrequent greeting among the old women, with a variety of responses: "Yes, I've been on this cabbage soup diet and I have lost twelve pounds"; "I wish I had, it must be this top." An old woman walks into the room. "Look at her," says Josie. "She has lost about thirty pounds." "I hear she has been on a hard-boiled egg diet" someone responds; another says "ugh!" Mostly, the old women do not accost one another saying "You've gained weight!" but they do talk about the overweight or weight gain of self or others. Kathi says of one old woman: "She told me what she weighs, and it is astonishing." Harriet's weight and constant dieting was a subject of conversation for the decade between 60 and 70.

Diet and food talk make up a not-insubstantial portion of old women's conversation, in what has been referred to elsewhere as "display" (Warren, 1998). At a luncheon, Candy, who is slender at 60, says "no" to the bread and butter that is being passed, saying, "I have gained a pound and I need to get it off." A 75-year-old friend says, "Hmph. I have gained more than a pound and I can't seem to do anything to get it off." If an old woman is fat, the norm is that she must talk about what she is doing to lose weight; most overweight old women—like Harriet—obey, engaging in food, diet and/or exercise talk and display.

Public accolades accrue to the women who have lost weight and those who are ever-slender. "You look wonderful!" refers to being well-dressed, well made up, and well-coiffed, but it is also code for a slender body. Although the compliments flow for weight loss and slenderness, there is an undercurrent of competition.

Kathi: "Caroline lost a pair of size 2 pants somewhere around here."
Eve: "Size 2?"
Kathi: "Yes."
Eve: "Bitch!!!!"

For the old woman, "looking nice" is enhanced by adornment in the form of accessories and jewelry—a designer handbag and some sapphire and diamond earrings. Simone de Beauvoir says that

> Elderly women['s] . . . sexuality now shows only in their dress, their jewelry and ornaments; and in the pleasure they take in male society . . . they are touched by the attentions that show they are still women in men's eyes.
>
> (1972: 349)

Simone de Beauvoir has perhaps never been in a group of people for whom the "only" is a bit of an overstatement. As we will see in Part III, sexuality among the old women may take more direct forms than dress and male attention in public. But still, among the more privileged old women, expensive jewelry and accessories are in some sense a distraction from an aging body and its parts. An emerald necklace draws the eye to itself rather than the neck wattles it adorns. Large ruby earrings focus the gaze away from drooping earlobes.

Our culture does not as yet have a cure for old age but bulges with cures for unbearable weight, most of which revolve around the ancient ideals of moderation and self-control. The Greek, Roman and medieval elder "exemplified the virtues of moderation, balance, and self-control, in the bodily arenas of eating, drinking and sexuality" (Demaitre, 1990), setting the foundation for today's stress on moderation. Moderate diet, moderate drinking (no moderate smoking, though), moderate exercise, moderate weight, all moderated for a healthier (and perhaps longer) old age. We seek to halt the progress of osteoporosis with enforced posture change, we go to the gym daily to combat the descent of muscle into hanging flab, we bike, play tennis or golf, or run for weight mainte-nance, and we walk to keep our knees from locking into immobility. All healthy, all valorized culturally.

Dieting preoccupies some of the old women. Esther talks episodically about being on a diet, while her weight yo-yos from fairly normal to slender. Maggy makes no public comments about eating. But if asked, she will tell you that she is a lifetime member of a weight loss group and goes to meetings and weigh-ins. She adds:

> "I started gaining weight after menopause. I had always been a size 10; when I reached a size 14 and my clothes were tight, I decided to do something. . . . I joined this group and lost forty pounds in a month. I have kept all but six or eight pounds off for fifteen years, and I am a size 8."

But the slender body is as liable to some of the effects of aging as the fat. Maggy adds:

> "I hate aging. Everything is starting to bag and sag, and I have a tummy no matter what I do."

Many old women diet, some exercise, others do both. They can be seen on the sunny Southern California streets, bicycling or running. Many go to the gym. Old women who exercise on a routine basis sig-nal their commitment with adornment: sleeveless shirts, shorts, tights, gym shoes, gym bags—all on a slender body. At 60, Bridget goes to the gym daily for spinning and other exercises. She wears sleeveless shirts and shorts to show off her muscular legs and arms, of which she is very proud. She said: "I was going to get a short dress for the New Year's Eve ball, to show off my legs, but I ended up wearing a long one that I wore twenty years ago"—a humble brag, telling us that she is still as slender as she was twenty years ago. Anna still goes to the gym every day. She exchanged the sleeveless shirts for sleeves some years ago but looks trim in her gym clothes. She is a neighbor with whom we have exchanged pleasantries from time to time during the last fifteen years; every time we have had an exchange she has mentioned the gym. Her husband says, "She will die on the floor of that gym." Body, gym, life, for some of the old women—but not as much as Ernestine Shepherd the body builder.

Swimming—in pools or on the beach—is recommended as a way of getting exercise for those who find it difficult, because of knee problems or other issues, to go to the gym or ride bikes. But swimming requires wearing a swimsuit, which for fat old women is not something they are willing to do. Jolene says: "I am not going to get into the pool and swim, any more than I will put on a swimsuit when we all go on cruises. But I do water aerobics." Carol "Don't you have to wear a swimsuit for that?" Jolene, "Yes, but we are all fat old women in our class." One fat old woman we know is willing to swim with known others in a local pool. But for all old women, fat women, and old fat women there is the issue of appearing in public in a swimsuit. As Weiner (2016) notes:

> there are women out there who don't wear swimsuits. They don't go to the beach. They basically forego summer, and the camera, because they hate the way they look.

And with good reason. Dani Mathews, a former Playboy model, was prosecuted after she published a body-shaming snapshot of an overweight 70-year-old woman showering in a gym.

Old/fat women have varying takes on wearing a swimsuit to swim or go to the beach. One fat woman says that "I avoid swimming altogether, and it's actually one of my favorite things to do" (Weiner, 2016). For decades Carol would only appear in a swimsuit if nobody she knew was present. However, she recently found swim shorts with coverage to the knees and a rasher with coverage up to the neck and down to the elbows—and wore it on a cruise with friends. Other fat/old women, like Jennifer Weiner herself, wear swimsuits or go to the beach no matter what; she has inspired some old/fat women to return to swimsuited beachgoing. Thin old women may cover up their abdomens, arms or legs when they go to the beach or pool. Maggy wears a medium-sleeved T-shirt over her swimsuit in the hot tub.

By the time the old woman is 70, it is not just excess weight that is revealed by swimwear; it is the sagging of the skin. Karyn says of her upcoming beach vacation that she is not looking forward to it because of

> the reality of having a beach vacation where a swimsuit is required. My swimsuit days are over! I'll be wearing some old swimsuits with sarongs. That's the only way I want to be seen. And big hats and sunglasses.

Karyn is as slender as she has been for decades ("some old swimsuits"), but it is likely that her upper arms are sagging and wrinkling, and probably her lower arms, thighs and torso as well. For women like Karyn, the marketplace is ready to provide solutions that include "modest swimwear" ranging from full coverage birkini for Muslim women to long-sleeve rashers that cover the upper arms, chest and neck area and swim shorts that hide the thighs.

There are many body-related emotions discussed in these chapters, including shame, fear and sadness. The wearing of swimsuits by fat/old women can result in shame and humiliation. Women are ashamed to be old as they look into the mirror. They are humiliated by the possibility of being photographed in a swimsuit—or, worse, naked in a gym shower. So they avoid the public eye by staying away from the swimsuit, the gym shower, the beach, the pool and the camera. The young woman who photographed the old woman in the gym shower has her hand over her mouth and her eyes wide and horrified in the snapchat. The caption: "If I cannot unsee this then you can't either." Body shaming by others is, to the self, humiliation—"I cannot show my face" its distillatory phrase.

Many of the old women engage in sports such as tennis and golf. These activities are seen as "good for" the functioning of the aging body, keeping it toned and perhaps slender. And they give pleasure to some (if not all) the women who engage in them. Having to give them up, piece by piece and one by one, means giving up part of the pleasure of the senses. The Catch-22 for the old woman is that if she does not give up tennis—say—and its pleasures, she will suffer from arm, wrist, back, shoulder or hand pain. We know some old people in their eighties and nineties who still play tennis, bike or run—but none have continued competitively past their sixties (we realize that old people do still compete, but not the ones we know). Giving up first competition, then the activity itself, cuts off phantom limbs of the old self, especially the woman who was athletic in her youth. Lee writes of her body as if in a poem:

> I played tennis but lost my partners.
> I loved volleyball but it became too strenuous.
> I have always been a walker and continue to walk.

Absent running, tennis, running, golf and the gym, there is always the possibility of taking a walk—at least for now. The old women walk in temperate climes on the beach and in the streets. In inclement weather, they walk around Walmart or IKEA. Virtually everyone walks, here and now—except for those whose disabilities preclude walking. When we see old women in wheelchairs, pushed by spouses or caregivers, we wonder if, and how soon, it will come to that for us.

Carol: "I don't feel like walking much anymore. Even when my knees and hips don't hurt, my body feels awkward walking, as if I have been put together, joint by joint, by someone drunk."

Walking may be one of the "natural" ways of organizing the aging body, but it has been supplemented by the medical-measurement fever of our time: "Fitbits" are on many an elderly arm in our community. Marian, 60, takes the lead in challenging Lucy, 68, and others to keep up with her, and they try to do it—and to out-number her step-count as often as they can. The subtheme of the Fitbit is a competition to see who can remain slender between the women's sixtieth and eightieth years. Lucy says, "I could walk nonstop for a year and I would still be fatter than Marian." Marian is thin; Lucy is slender.

More interventionist methods of weight control include everything from diet pills to bariatric surgery. Several women report keeping their weight down in previous decades with (then) readily available drugs similar to speed. Annette says,

> "When I was in my twenties I took pills prescribed by my doctor. I took them for ten years, and I took other pills to go to sleep. Since they were prescribed I did not know they were bad for me. I took those drugs again in my 50s but found I could only tolerate them for a couple of weeks."

We know no old women who have had bariatric surgery; the surgical body modification of choice is liposuction. The old women we know report liposuction procedures on many parts of their bodies: abdomen, thighs, hips. Some of the Southern California women go across the border to Mexico for the procedure, since it is—in the words of one liposuction patient—"very expensive." Marlene said that she was going to have liposuction "again" before a beach holiday, but then added:

> "I am actually joking. I had it twice. Once I had fat taken off my thighs. It was expensive, but I only lost three-quarters of a pound. The next time I had some taken out of my side and back below my waist. That was expensive too. Trouble is, now the flesh on my sides and back sort of pooches over in folds."

These fat-fighting procedures reflect a vast marketplace for the losing of unbearable weight, from surgery to diet books to gyms to pills. The same is true for those who are unwilling or unable to be thin; the marketplace can provide women with everything from plus-size clothing to extra-large shoes. This "fat" market is full of advice: to love our own bodies whatever size they are and wear those tight jeans and short tops if we want to—in any color. Although perhaps when we are 17 rather than 70.

This "fat is fab" marketplace gets its clientele from both mad-as-hell and self-accepting fat women. The nonprofit National Association for the Advancement of Fat People (NAAFA) reports on and advocates for the civil rights of fat people and keeps track of medical and employment issues that affect fat people. There are also associations (nowadays found on the internet), such as "Fat Admirers" and "Chubby Chasers," composed of members seeking the sexual company of fat women. However, the organizations typically focus on fat women and men in the decades of employment and marriage rather than retirement and old age and are of little interest to the old women. Kay, a recent widow at 75, weighs perhaps 350 lbs. She says, "I am lonely, and I would like to get back into dating"—but so far as we can tell from the dating websites, FAs are in search of younger women.

Feminists exhort young and old women to accept themselves as they are, whether they are gray haired, wrinkled or fat—and, indeed, there are some women, young and old, who do accept their bodies. Others have adopted the moral principle of self-acceptance and cultural refusal but are ambivalent in practice. Debora Spar (2016) points out that the women in her social circles are "uniformly thin" and that she "would stand out as an anomaly" if she were to age gracefully. "Everyone is better off if nobody tummy-tucks or uses Botox, but once anyone starts, it gets harder to pull back from the practice." Thus come the ultimate bodily alterations: the tummy-tuck or bariatric surgery.

The public body is more than height and weight. The clothed, public body also shows (off) parts of the body that may cleave to the ideal—or not: breasts, belly and buttocks. Breasts, server of feasts for small babies, are also sexual and cosmetic aspects of the thin, normal or fat body. For couples, they are part of nakedness; for the observer, breasts are contained in bras, hidden under clothing or partially bared with a décolletage. Some old women have had mastectomies and reconstructive surgery in past years; others have had breast augmentation; a few have had breast reduction surgery. But whatever is done—or not—to the breasts, there is a difference between the youthful breasts of the young body and the gravity-prone dugs of the old.

Breast augmentation is the most common of the 15.6 million "minimally invasive" and surgical procedures done in the United States in 2016 (www.plasticsurgery.org). We do not know of any women between 70 and 80 who have had breast augmentation, but we know several who had them earlier in life and a few younger ones who want the surgery. Viola, who is almost 60, and Nikki, who is half her age, both want augmentation, but it is financially out of their reach. In the meantime, there are other solutions: creams that promise to enlarge breast tissue and padded or push-up bras. Lily says that her breasts were tiny when she was younger, but now "they are just the right size, although I sometimes wear a slightly padded bra." A few old women had breast reductions when they were younger. Annette says:

> "My breasts started growing when I was ten, and by the time I was fourteen they were quite large and hung down. I had to pull them up by the bra straps, and I did not want to get in the shower at school with the other girls after gym. When I was eighteen I had a breast reduction, and by the time I was twenty-eight, and quite thin, I had small breasts."

However, with age, weight gain and gravity, Annette's breasts became large and pendulous again. Breasts increase in size as women age, especially if they gain weight.

When we old women were young, adult women's bodies were thickly corseted from breasts to thigh, with breasts pulled up and out into stiff pyramids. Clothing revealed the breast as a full cone without visible nipples. Today, a more "natural" look is commonplace among the young, with breasts in place more or less as they are, held in by thin bras, if at all. If the old woman's breasts are in their natural place, they are observed and commented on.

> We are sitting at a table with the usual group. May walks in. She is wearing a see-through white top. Her breasts reach to her waist, with bronze-colored nipples pointing downward. Eve says,

"Look at that." Nikki: "I wonder if she has Alzheimer's." Carol: "She doesn't seem to be wearing a bra." Viola: "I think she is wearing a bra, it is just thin."

The displaying of old breasts in public, the visibility of nipples and not wearing a bra under a see-through top are so violative of local norms that they either are not believed to be possible or are seen as a symptom of disease.

Breasts "in the wrong place"—nearer the waist than halfway between underarms and elbows—are more common than bra-less breasts among old women. Jennie, 73, was wearing a new blouse and said:

"I don't like the way this blouse looks. What is wrong with it?" Carol reached under the blouse, grabbed the strap, and pulled up the left breast about three inches, repeating the process with the right strap and breast. "There. The blouse looks great."

In her husband's words, Jennie's (public) breasts had been returned to "their correct place" in the body's public outline. After a few weeks, however, Jennie had returned her breasts to her waist, complaining that the "other way" was "too uncomfortable."

In Chapter 1, we were introduced to the idea that leathery cleavage is horrible and even frightening. Olds (2016: 27), in an "Ode of Withered Cleavage" recounts her horror, when young, that an old woman would appear in public with her cleavage showing. The poem expresses an ironic disbelief that anyone would show off her labyrinth of grooves and ruts. But, in sports and at formal events, the old women do. All but the most modest swimsuits expose women's cleavage, as does some tennis and golf attire. Evening attire is also often designed to show cleavage, and the old women do so at formal events:

SueAnn is dressed for the ball. Diamonds glitter at her throat and on her wrists and fingers. She is wearing shiny silver high heels and a snug black dress that sweeps to the floor. The dress has long sleeves, and the neckline plunges to reveal cleavage.

On more everyday occasions, the show of cleavage is less common and may become the object of observation and comment among the old women.

> Kitty walks by LouAnn's table at lunchtime. She is wearing a skirt and a peasant top with a low neckline that shows her cleavage. LouAnn sniffs, turns her head, and tsks to her husband who is sitting next to her.

Cleavage is a contested terrain for revelation or cover-up; another is the upper arms and underarms. While most women—old and young—shave their underarm hair, only some old women are willing to wear sleeveless clothing, no matter what the summer temperature or summer fashion. Shoulders, too, may be covered or bared. As we write, a few of the old women are wearing the "cold shoulder" top, a peasant blouse with bared shoulders; the style was adopted by Eve in her eighties and Wilma in her seventies.

Old women generally do not bare their abdomens, either by wearing two-piece swimsuits or adopting visible navel rings. A youthful abdomen features a taut, flat, perhaps even concave belly from waist to pubis. Not so the belly of the old woman, unless she is thin to the point of anorexia or muscled to the point of a body builder. Old women who reveal their abdomens are objects of derision or pity. A photograph of Ivana Trump in a bikini at age 68 contrasts with the body she had when she married Donald Trump—and the bodies of his next two wives when he married them. That photograph probably does not contrast with the aging body of Donald Trump himself, but in a world of gender this seems not to matter. Barbara Eden, 78-year-old former star of "I Dream of Jeannie," can fit into her decades-ago navel-hinting costume without a bulging belly—but the wrinkled skin of that belly has the commentator describing her as "brave" for baring it.

Slender old women such as Maggy may have a "tunkey"—an abdomen that is not flat but can be disguised by wearing an untucked shirt, or a jacket. But the fat belly, despite efforts to hide it with artfully draped clothing, is visible in the outline of the old woman's body; she may accept it or attempt to modify it through those "natural" diet and exercise methods, or she may resort to artifice. Corsets were the nineteenth and twentieth century method of coping with the flabby belly. Liposuction is one twenty-first century equivalent. Several women in their seventies and eighties described their earlier liposuction procedures but expressed no inclination to repeat the process. Another solution to a sagging abdomen is the lower body lift, a surgical procedure that has increased 3,973% since 2000 (www.plasticsurgery.org). Although there are many fat women with bellies, it is a rare woman who revels in her parts. In her poem "My Belly," Marjorie Agosin (Cole and Winkler, 1994) rejoices in her wide belly and pendulous breasts—her 70-year-old body "a good companion."

Buttocks, in old age, are subject to the same forces of gravity that affect breasts, bellies (and earlobes). The ideal of the youthful body is buttocks that are full, high and firm—but not TOO full, high and firm. Some old people had ideal buttocks in their youth, others not so much; very few retain ideal buttocks in old age. Recently Kathi and Carol were walking behind an old woman in a grocery store. She was thin and bent over, with white hair and wrinkles, wearing tight black pants; her buttocks were as shapely as those of a 20-year-old. We looked at each other and voiced the same thought: "Great butt!"

Old women who are not keen on their buttocks can avail themselves of devices and medical procedures that round, shape and lift their behinds. The American Society of Plastic Surgeons reports that the number of buttock lifts increased by 252% between 2000 and 2015 (www.plasticsurgery.org). One of the old women admits to having had a buttock lift when she was younger; at least one other wears a device that lifts and pads her otherwise sagging buttocks. But gravity is, eventually, not to be defied.

Only the fairly well-off and privileged are able to have the surgical procedures that change our bodies as we age. And a lot of the old women have them. For most of the women that we know, whatever degree of intervention they have had constitutes the norm, and they are perfectly willing to talk about their procedures, dermatologists and cosmetic surgeons. For some, like the women in Spar's social circles, an ideological opposition to age intervention pushes the intervention underground.

> Everyone . . . is doing it, and very few are confessing, a fact that in some ways is more disturbing than the surge in the surgeries themselves. Because not only are we nipping, suctioning, and using hormones, but we are also feeling embarrassed about it, and lying. Neither of which was really the point of women's liberation.
>
> (Spar, 2016)

But we do engage in bodily interventions because our bodies are no longer fit (as we see it) for public display. Excess weight is unbearable throughout a lifetime, as Bordo has shown us. For the aging woman, it is one—arguably still the most important one—of a series of bodily changes that grow increasingly unbearable. Psychology tells us that we feel, inside, much as we did at 13, or 30. But our outsides begin to unmatch ourselves to the point that our bodies are no longer ourselves. Only last year we wrote:

Carol: "I have one part of my body that seems normal to me: my two calves, below my kneecaps (which have seen very hard times) to above my ankle. Everything else is wretched."
Kathi: "I don't like my neck, or my upper arms, but that is about it so far."

One year later:

Kathi: "There is a proliferation of wrinkles on my face and over my whole body. The changes in my skin are astonishing."
Carol: "Those two normal calves? Gone, girl."

This unbearable weight of our bodies that are not ourselves is why we diet, exercise, dye our hair, wear makeup and have face-lifts. Even unto four score and ten.

PART III
THE BODY WITH OTHERS

6

THE HALL OF MIRRORS

Aging in Sexual and Social Relationships

Almost all the women whose voices we have heard so far are in relationships with others—significant others, families, friends. Some are married or partnered, while a few are single. Many have families: adult children, grandchildren and great-grandchildren, siblings and (rarely) very aged parents. All have friends and acquaintances and move around in a world of strangers. The hall of mirrors reflects all of us: we see ourselves and are seen; others see us and are seen, in an endless sequence. We see our bodies naked and adorned. We see not only our future aging selves in those older than us but our past aging in those younger—and they see us.

The metaphor of the mirror is common among those of us who write about aging. The "mirror stage" of old age begins

> When older individuals look in the mirror, see themselves in photographs, or catch a glimpse of themselves in a shop window, [and] they can experience feelings of alienation from the image that is projected back at them.
>
> (Brooks, 2017: 70)

Within our social circles, there is a collective mirroring of not only the culture's but the local "social mores, expectations, attitudes and behaviors reflected in them" (Brooks, 2017: 141). This local mirror varies by what part of the country the woman lives in and how she lives her daily life.

We first encountered our local hall of mirrors at a dinner party with the two of us, in our seventies; Clarice and Benny, in their eighties; and Earl and Candy, approaching their sixties:

> Earl and Candy are excited about the New Year's Eve party they are going to. Candy says, "They will have a band, and a champagne toast at midnight." Carol responds, "We always see the ball drop at midnight in New York then go to bed, we can't stay up past 9:30, if that." Eve says, "We do too." Candy: "Oh no, you've got to go with us. We'll get a table. It's only one night and, you know, YOLO."

The 60—year-olds did not attempt to persuade the 80-year-olds to go to the party—they could see 80, as if in a far-off mirror, but they saw us closer up. We, seventies, looked at Earl and Candy and saw ourselves at 60, when we did, indeed, stay at New Year's Eve parties until midnight.

We mirror our own and each other's aging bodies among friends, family, intimates and strangers. Our bodies are clothed in public and private and unclothed in private. The most proximate of bodily observation and contact is sex, in all its iterations. In our households, with intimate others, we share the various aging aspects of the private body described in Part I, from farting and belching to sleeping and snoring. And it is in our private households that some of us, eventually, become disabled and take on the props of old age, beginning with a cane, then a walker, a wheelchair, an adult diaper. And so it goes.

But all is not lost. A few aspects of the aging body may bring relief. One is the absence of periods after menopause, as we saw in Chapter 2. Some of us had periods that did not involve a lot of pain, stress or blood (Kathi)—but they were still periods. Others had all kinds of problems, from heavy periods that lasted two weeks to painful conditions such as endometriosis (Carol). When asked if not having periods is a relief, Annette said:

> "OMG, yes. You know what endometriosis is, right? There is so much menstrual blood that it spills over into the abdomen and

grabs on, and it can migrate to other places as well. I used to have so much blood that I could go through pads and tampons in a few minutes."

There are writings that celebrate menstruation and the fertility that it symbolizes; rightly so. But we are very, very glad that it is gone.

Another gift bestowed by an old body is not being verbally or physically harassed by strange men in public or by our bosses at work or school. Donald Trump would not be interested in grabbing our pussies. In our youth, most of us experienced the unwanted eyes, hands and body parts of men invading our spaces. Men—not only strangers, but also relatives, family friends—touched us unasked, displayed their genitals to us, and spoke of things we did not want to hear.

Kathi: "When I was fourteen a teacher grabbed one of my buttocks. All through junior high the baseball coach hugged and kissed me and made me very uncomfortable. When I was nineteen, visiting a museum in San Francisco, a man walked up to me and grabbed a breast. When I was a graduate student, working at a computer, a senior professor came up behind me, grabbed my shoulders, and tried to kiss me on the cheek. That stayed with me for decades, actually until retirement."

Carol: "When I was about six, I played in the woods with friends (those were the days when our parents let us wander). One day we came across a naked man in a clearing, doing what we could not imagine then and do not have to now. We ran for our lives. When I was ten, a family friend was bouncing me on his knee, and suddenly began to slobber on my mouth with his. I jumped off and ran. When I was twelve, I was in a ski lift cage with a cousin, who tried to kiss me. I slapped him. I think I would not have slapped him if we had not been trapped in that ski lift. When I was about nineteen, I was with a friend in the Acropolis; we turned a corner and there was a man masturbating. When I was in my thirties, I was walking in Los Angeles when a man stopped in front of me to tie his shoe and allow his genitals to fall out of his shorts."

As we grow old, and perhaps fat, our bodies become uninviting to the potential molester. When Jessica Leech, now 74, accused Donald Trump of groping her on a plane, his response was: "Believe me, she would not be my first choice" to sexually assault. Of a younger but not slender woman, he said, "Check out her Facebook page, you'll understand" his claim that he did not assault her (Wright, 2016).

On the other hand, the old women are at times harassed by some of the old men; we know several such men. Maggy says of James, who is in his early seventies, that "he has sexually harassed me for twenty years." Clarissa agrees, "Me too—I have known him for twenty years, too."

> At the bar, James says to Clarissa, "Why don't you get naked for me?" She laughs and says, "If I did you would be very sorry."
>
> At a party, James walks by Carol holding a hot dog out. "Where do you want me to put it?" he says; Carol replies, "You can shove it up your ass."
>
> By the bar, James asks Kathi "Are you going to wear a one- or two-piece swimsuit on the cruise?" Kathi: "A birkini," mimicking coverage from head to toe. On another occasion, he pulled Carol's V-neck sweatshirt zipper down about two inches to expose cleavage.

And there are others.

> Alf, who is in his late eighties, is sitting at the bar next to Kathi. He begins rubbing her back. Wanda says "Stop that" and slaps his hand. Alf says, "I love feeling girls' bra straps."
>
> Kathi and Carol are looking for seats at a Super Bowl party. Maurice leers at Kathi and says, "You can come sit on my lap."
>
> Simon, who is in his late seventies, roams around eyeing the women in the bar. As he passes us, he says, "Don't you love me anymore?"

In the private club where these events occurred, some men, both old and young, have been formally charged with sexual harassment, and some have been forced to resign. James and the others, however, have not and likely will not be pursued. We old women are no longer fearful of assault or of threats to our careers, since we are all retired. We can talk back, and we can give as good as we get. We are not vulnerable in the ways that the women of #MeToo and the entertainment industry are, although we do note one similarity: sexual harassment seems to almost always take place when the woman involved does not have a male partner in the vicinity. As Marlene says, "Of course Simon does not bother me! Louis [her husband] is always standing right there!"

Many of these old men have wives and girlfriends who are (presumptively) in sexual relationships with them. Many of the old women have partners or spouses, but others, from menopause to 100, do not. For women around the age of menopause, the search for sexual partners may be successful; Pepper Schwartz (2007) recounts her quest for sex and romance after the break-up of an over twenty-year-old marriage. She did a lot of body work to accomplish her goals, from losing weight and exercising to hair, skin and nail improvement (if this had been ten years later, she would have been focusing on her eyebrows as well). Older women who want to "date"—to get to know a stranger or old acquaintance, and embark, perhaps, on a sexual adventure or new relationship—are daunted by imagining their bodies, buttocks and breasts with another body. Once into the late sixties and onward, the body resists remaining firm and inviting. As Friedan (1993) points out, old women who don't have sexual partners may refrain from "dating" because they do not want to be naked with another. She quotes a researcher who says that older women

> feel it is obscene to feel and express sensual and sexual feelings if they are . . . wrinkled, gray haired, fat, skinny and sagging. . . . Women feel undesirable as they see their bodies as no longer firm and supple, but old and not luscious.
>
> (p. 268)

Although a number of the old women have found new mates among the old men in their neighborhoods and clubs, others have not. And some widows do not want to. Sylvia said, "I had a wonderful sex life in and outside of marriage, and I am not looking anymore." Clarissa is tall, slender and attractive, with long blond hair, widowed after thirty years of marriage, although she too was not looking to date. "I had the most wonderful sexual relationship and that is that." Clarissa has resisted all attempts from friends to "fix her up." But after five years she found companionship with the man who was the best man at her wedding. We found this to be a common pattern among old women who did find new partners: they reconnected with men from their past, from best men to old high school boyfriends.

In this online world, the old woman willing to navigate those waters may find sex and romance. At the age of 67, after thirty years of widowhood and near-celibacy, Jane Juska put an ad into the *New York Review of Books* that said she would "like to have a lot of sex with a man I like" (Rees Jones, 2015: 17). She eventually received sixty-three responses from—and had sex with—men aged 32 to 82. A couple of the old women we know have acquired dates through internet dating services, although they face the well-known problem of men seeking younger partners. And Juska had to move from her wish for one "man I like" to the reality of a sequence of men.

Other old women, alone, would like to be fixed up with a partner but face low statistical odds. Old women are much more likely to live alone than old men: 23% of men 75 and older live alone—and 46% of women. Among those 80 years old or older, 60% of men are married but only 17% of women. (Span, 2016). The emotional toll of loneliness may be exacerbated, for the less well off, by economic hardship. And there is nobody to share the pain. Men may have some of the same concerns, in addition to possible problems with their "Pecker"—although, unlike Maximianus in the fifth century, contemporary men have several medical options for obtaining and maintaining erections.

As noted in earlier chapters, some feminists, such as Germaine Greer, claim that they—and postmenopausal women in general—are free from sexual desire. Some of the old women agree. When asked about sex, Karyn said dismissively, "Who cares?" Some husbands or partners do care. Meredith has been married for six years to her 80-year-old third husband. She says:

> I have absolutely no interest in sex. But if one is married to a virile man, as I am, you have to go along with it. If we never had sex it would not damage our relationship from my point of view, but it would from his point of view.

Meredith describes herself as "slender," so a fat body is not part of her sexual disinterest. Meredith and other wives accommodate their husbands sexually, whether they themselves are interested or not. Sexual openness to husbands is seen as one way to keep them or as part of their marital "job." Describing a very recent surgical facial procedure, LouAnn says:

> "They took the fat out of my thighs and put it in my face."
> "How?" "They put it in a centrifuge and whirled it around."
> "Do your thighs hurt?"
> "Well, they look like I have been going at my job too hard!"

Like Meredith—and unlike many of the old women—LouAnn's "job" may be (to her) complicated by an aging face, but it is unaffected by being overweight.

In some marriages, the cessation of sex has less to do with the woman—her weight or age—but with the husband's physical or mental state. Lee says that

> "Sex left my life many years ago because of physical problems with my husband (he is 90). We went to counselors and therapists and finally decided to forget about it. I am sure that there is an underlying anger in both of us—but we muddle through."

Lee adds—despite her constant pain from arthritis and her husband's spinal issues—that "both of us have no problems with our body. We accept the changes and go forward."

An old, fat body may or may not affect an old woman's willingness to be sexual with a partner or spouse, and it may or may not affect her sexual partner's response to her. A husband cannot prevent a wife growing old, but he can—and many do—demand that she stay thin. Inge and Ham are in their early seventies. Ham comments if Inge consumes something he thinks she should not—a piece of bread, some butter: "You don't need that." Marcia, 70, says that her husband "will not let me eat potato chips, so I hide them." Gray or white hair may not be enticing, either; Kreamer (2007: 198) says that in her survey twice as many men as women thought that women who had gray or white hair were "letting themselves go"—a phrase often used with reference to fat women. Lisa was pleased that her husband liked her newly gray hair.

We do not observe the quantity or quality of couples' bodies and sexuality but hear about it from time to time in general conversation.

> We are discussing how old men have nice legs without wrinkles, pointing out Jeff's smooth legs under his shorts—he is 85. Emma, his wife, says *sotto voce* to Kathi: "Yes, but men have that awful ear hair, and nose hair, and those ugly wiggly things of theirs."

Nicole hoped that her third husband would remain uninterested in intercourse after prostate surgery because "sex hurts after menopause." Ex-husbands are fair game. LouAnn said that her second husband was "into porn," and "I just hated it. He made me go see 'Deep Throat' and I left after ten minutes and waited in the foyer." She says of her current husband: "I wonder why he is trying to get me drunk. Does he want some action? I am so much better if I am not drunk." Some women in their seventies and older have experienced improvement in their sex lives or orgasmic capacity. Alice says of her second husband that his approach to sex was "whim, wham, thank you, ma'am." Her third husband was, in her words, "good at sex." Lily says that she has "raging hormones—how can it be that sex seems to get better and better?"

There is a cultural and economic context to old women's sexuality. Sandberg (2015) contrasts the (older) image of the "asexual oldie" with the (newer) "sexy seniors." She points out that these Western cultural themes can inhibit old women's interest in sex, which Chapter 1 illustrated for premodern times. But the "sexy senior" trope casts as "unnatural" the old woman or man who is simply not interested in sex. For those who are interested, the marketplace can provide everything from sex toys to pharmaceuticals. Men are prescribed drugs that enable them to obtain and maintain erections. Tessa says that she and her 69-year-old husband "are able to have a gentle sex life, despite his enlarged prostate and with the aid of [pharmaceuticals]." At this time, there is no equivalent erectile stimulating drug for women, but there are various medications including estrogen skin creams for dryness or testosterone for "low libido" that may improve interest in sex and orgasmic function. We saw in Chapter 3 that Tessa takes HRT "for my general disposition, and for vaginal receptivity. . . . I also take Prozac, which gives me problems with orgasm. But then I use a vibrator."

The aging body in bed has issues beyond sex. Spouses and partners fart more, become incontinent with greater frequency and snore more. Couples who sleep in the same bed or in the same room may be troubled by all of these and more, sleep broken by the other's flatulence, snoring or rushing to the bathroom. Annette says, laughing, "It is like the dawn chorus in our bed in the morning, both of us sniffling and farting." Keith, 72, whose snoring is exacerbated by both aging and alcohol, says:

> "I am drinking less than I used to. For me, snoring is caused by drinking. And when I snore, Iris gets up to sleep in the other room. I don't want her to have to do that, so I am drinking less." His wife, Iris, adds, "I leave the room at 3.30 in the morning rather than 1:30" (laughter).

Eve wakes her husband up at night when she gets up to go to the bathroom. Snoring increases with age, so Eve's husband wakes her up when he snores. Married only six years, Eve and Bob are not yet willing to sleep in separate beds or rooms. But many couples who have been married a long time eventually separate at nighttime in order to ensure less-disturbed sleep. For sleep, after all, is one of the often-elusive joys of old age.

Outside the bedroom, the body is observed in interaction with household members and people outside the household. Implicit in earlier chapters is the theme of body policing: women controlling their weight, tweezing their chin hairs or putting on a bra. Body policing is also a function of partners and spouses and, to a lesser extent, family and friends. We have seen in earlier chapters how husbands police wives—and sometimes the reverse—for eating or drinking, often as a matter of weight control, although heart health is also sometimes invoked. We also saw how bothersome old age behaviors such as scratching are commented on by partners. One spouse polices the other's drinking to excess (Emerson, 2015); another complains that her partner needs a hearing test. When an overweight old woman reached for some bread at dinner, a male friend stopped her hand and said, "Friends don't let friends eat bread." Sometimes, body policing reminds the other of the dangers and difficulties of various activities: "Please don't lift that, it will hurt your shoulder"—the ever-present possibilities of pain and disability for the old woman.

Bob Emerson (2015) has written extensively about trouble in interpersonal relationships, including couples. He focuses on the troubling or troubled behavior of one spouse reacted to by the other, then either folding back on itself or continuing into realms of friendship circle advice, relationship therapy or medicalization. There are bodily troubles between spouses and partners, too. Emerson speaks several times of "drunken spouses," a condition at the intersection of body and behavior that can presumably occur at any age. The police function of couple-dom can extend beyond drunkenness to other aspects of the body. Kathi reprimands Carol for scratching her hands and fingers, remarking that "scratching your hands is an old person's behavior." Partners or spouses may be commented upon for not policing the other's body:

> We are sitting at a bar table when Joanna comes in. She turns away from us after saying hello, and we see the back of her head. She has a gray patch on the crown of her dyed-blond hair. Eve comments, "Her husband should make sure she does not go out looking like that."

Partners and spouses comment upon and police our cosmetic bodies as we get older. And this has a gendered dimension. Joanna's husband does not make sure she does not leave the house with her hair awry; Alice says her husband prefers her with short wigs rather than long; Lisa's husband is OK with her newly white hair. As we have seen, many husbands police their wives' weight, commenting on their eating habits. For same-sex couples, gender is doubly mirroring: we see ourselves and the other in the other and ourselves.

> Kathi and I are both applying makeup, looking in the bathroom mirror, darkening offending white eyebrow hairs. Kathi says, "It's a good thing that eyelashes don't turn white like eyebrows." Carol silently points to the two white hairs in her left eyelash.

One year later: Kathi is at the mirror plucking out offending white eyebrow hairs.

Partners and spouses of the old are faced not only with the cosmetic but with the functioning body of the other when we become sick or disabled. Old people are liable to the kinds of routine illnesses, such as influenza and upper respiratory infections, that plague people of every age. But as we get older "just a cold" becomes more of an ordeal, both for the sufferer and the caregiver. What starts with one person's upper respiratory infection (URI) becomes a collective burden; discomfort becomes pain.

Pain of all kinds and origins is likely to increase as we age. As we saw in the last chapter, for the individual pain may result in a loss of functioning, unpredictability and consequent depression. For the couple, pain may add another level of difficulty to the relationship, from interrupted sleep while a partner with hip pain tries to settle to snapping at the other because of lack of sleep or continual pain. The person in pain may be bedridden or unable to walk more than a few steps. At worst, one partner's general decline, with or without medical intervention, often requires the other partner to assume the role of a caregiver, with attendant consequences.

The newly minted caregiver must be there at all times, giving up any personal freedoms. The person in pain is depressed; the caregiver becomes depressed—a circle of dark mirrors. And all this is complicated by expectations; both the couples' habits and the gender-task division of labor in Western culture. The problems of couple caregivers and caregiving may be recognized in the gerontological literature on culture, but it is experienced firsthand by the old women or men. How does an 80-year-old woman help lift her 90-year-old husband into bed? Or conversely, how does a 90-year-old husband manage the household and the care of his 80-year-old wife? In those cases, home health care aids must be acquired and supervised. This is not only an issue of relative strength or home management skills, it is a gendered issue. In the 1930s–1950s, when most of the old women and men were raised, the man was responsible for the finances and the external household, from the backyard and garage to the public square, while the women cared for the household and children. The women lifted their children, and the men lifted heavy packages. The man might have lifted the woman over her threshold, but (with exceptions for couples in which the man was disabled) the woman did not lift the man. And most men did not do housework.

Many of the old women's first marriages played out in this cultural context. But divorce and remarriage, aging and pain, can change trajectories and expectations over time. The traditional gendered division of labor may no longer work because of the encroachment of age upon the body of the man, the woman or both. And caregiving can upend gendered expectations. The old woman rather than the old man—now in a wheelchair—must shovel the snow. The old man has to work out how to make chicken soup when his wife is ill. Folklore tells us that it takes a strong partnership or marriage for at least twenty years to enable a caregiver to tolerate this new world. Rae, who has been married for twenty-five years, says of her husband that "he has Parkinson's and he is going downhill. I am becoming his caregiver, and it will only get worse." We ask her if this is a problem. She shrugs her shoulders: "That is just the way it is."

We have seen many marriages between old people in the past decades, from fifty- and sixty-year unions to five- and six-year third or fourth marriages. In the more recent arrangements, the couple is as likely as not to remain unmarried while living together. Both have

resources—pensions, houses, and offspring—and they want their individual resources to go to their own offspring. The marriage of old men
to younger women is referred to as the "nurse for a purse" bargain, some
of the old men literally finding their nurse/wives among the caregivers attending to their first wife's terminal illnesses. Several of the old
women are with younger men who were in their employ (in three cases)
as gardeners, pool cleaners or drivers. A handyman for a purse.

Ruby and Sam have been together for eighteen years; the third marriage for her, the second for him. Fifteen years ago they were both
healthy and traveled a lot. Ruby cooked and took care of the inside of
the house (with the help of a housekeeper), while Sam was very handy
with gardening and home maintenance. Now, Ruby has not changed
much, but Sam's health has deteriorated considerably. He is unable
to help with routine chores, which angers Ruby—although "I know I
should not be mad at him, it is not his fault, but I am." Ruby continues
part-time work although she could retire; Sam is around the house all
day, "doing nothing," and she does not want to be with him constantly.

Clarice and Benny have been married for thirty years, a second
marriage for each; they are both in their early eighties. Because of eye
problems, Clarice has very little sight. But she does not use a cane, and
she navigates her friendship network and activities with Benny always
at her side, holding her elbow if necessary. They are always cheerful
and smiling. We asked Benny, once, if he wanted to join us for dinner,
because Clarice was home sick. He said, "Thanks, but I am going to get
right home to be with my lady." As of now, Benny has to do much of the
cooking, cleaning and housework (or hire services), but as yet he has not
had to do bed and body work.

Francie and her husband are in their mid-seventies and have been
married for twenty-five years. They spent half the year in Europe, skiing
and playing golf. She could still ski or play golf if she wanted to, but he
is confined to a wheelchair after a rapid decline in health that left him
with dementia and incontinent. With tears in her eyes, she says that so
far she has refused to put him into a residential facility because "you just
don't give up on people—but it is difficult for me when I have to lift
him and when he is incontinent." Sometimes his male caregiver wheels

him around the streets; at other times she gets him in and out of the car and wheels him into the club for dinner. In time, he became more difficult with dementia and more incontinent and entered a nursing home, where he died one year later.

Phyllis, 70, is caring for her husband Joe, disabled by MS; they have been married for twenty years. When we talked to Phyllis one evening, she was at a table and her husband was propped up on a barstool, his arm bandaged from shoulder to wrist.

> Kathi asked what happened. Phyllis said, "He fell again. He refuses to use his walker, or a cane. He just gets right up out of bed, and falls down. I can't get him back up. I have to call the paramedics." She rolls her eyes.

Like the women who stumble around because they can no longer wear contact lenses and won't wear glasses, refusing the props of old age can lead to falls and other disasters and make caregivers' work more difficult.

Not all old couples can cope with bodily caregiving; even if they have had a long marriage, that marriage might not have been a strong one. Sylvia and Brian, frequently quarrelsome and at odds, were both in their late sixties when Brian developed dementia. Sylvia denied that he had a medical problem, insisting that he was "doing it on purpose" when he wrecked the car or got lost on his way home. One day:

> We are out for a walk. We see Brian and ask him if he would like to come over for a bit. He says yes. He is filthy and starving. He tells us that Sylvia sends him out of the house for hours at a time. He says that earlier that day she had thrown a can of tomatoes at him that hit him on the side of the head and pushed him into a table loaded with glasses. We ask him if he wants to stay with us, and he says no, he is too afraid of Sylvia to leave. We had known that she isolated him and abused him emotionally, but not about the physical abuse.

We tried for two years to get a response from bureaucracies responsible for elder welfare. One of them stopped invoking privacy laws, listened to us, and got him out of the house into a nursing home—something that Sylvia had refused to do because of the financial bite it would have taken from his income (she had none). Brian died of the complications of dementia at the age of 70. Sylvia died of lung cancer and other conditions before her seventieth birthday.

Some old people do not need the caregiving of bed and body work, but their everyday lives are affected by chronic or acute pain. Pain affects intimate relationships in several ways, including depression, diminished functioning and, as Kathi says of Carol, "moaning and groaning" (Carol does not disagree). The more severe and chronic the pain, the greater the likelihood of depression, which then has an effect on the spouse and/or partner's mood and their everyday life—and the trajectory of the relationship. Severe and chronic pain generally affects a person's functioning, whether from migraine, rheumatoid arthritis or back spasms. The spouse slows down or halts her contribution to the couple's life, withdrawing from cooking, shopping or making beds. She can no longer join her partner on the tennis court, the swimming pool or a trip to Italy. This cycle of depression and lessened activity can lead to resentment on the part of the caregiver.

As these examples illustrate, trajectories of aging can occur in tandem for couples or take quite different turns for each. It is not surprising when a 90-year-old ages faster than his 70-year-old spouse, bringing age-related bodily relationship issues ranging from minor irritations of everyday life, such as an increase in snoring, to a rapid decline from ambulatory to wheelchair bound or continent to incontinent. But spouses or partners aged 70 and 72 can also age differentially, with one staying relatively youthful and the other declining at an accelerating rate—like Brian.

Kathi and Carol were aging similarly at 60, enjoying tennis, boogie boarding and other activities. By 70, Kathi had changed very little, but Carol had developed several painful conditions—in her knees in particular—that prevent or slow down movement. Kathi leaves the car and rushes into the grocery store well ahead of Carol, who is inching her way out of the car onto the pavement. She says, "Please slow down and wait for me." Kathi gets impatient and says, "I have to get used to the slowing down." These days, tennis is no more; instead, Kathi rides

her bicycle and occasionally plays golf. Our one attempt a tandem bik-
ing was unsuccessful, but Carol, who has never golfed, has discovered
the joys of riding along in a cart, watching Kathi play and enjoying the
scenery. When one partner's pain moves toward disability, the other is
forced to make adjustments—temporarily or permanently—in adopting a caregiving role. If the disability is temporary, cycles of irritation
and depression may come to an end. If the role of caregiver becomes
permanent, the disability may profoundly affect relationships.

Not all elderly spouses can tolerate the caregiver role, and, like Sylvia,
turn to abuse. This is true not only in situations of poverty but in situations of affluence like this one. Elder abuse is a recognized problem
in residential facilities for the old, but in the community it tends to be
hidden. Even when the abuse is not hidden, there appears to be little
one can do. In the case of Brian, calling the help line for elder abuse was
absolutely no help—we got a recorded message. The Health Insurance
Portability and Accountability Act (HIPAA), which deals with patient
privacy, turned out to be an impediment to intervention for suspected
elder abuse cases. There was nothing to be done with Brian's abuse until
someone within a hospital bureaucracy was persuaded to put HIPAA
aside and investigate the situation—our fate as old people may end up
in the hands of others and left to chance.

Some old women cannot afford home care, or insurance will not
pay; others have ample resources. And they are the lucky ones. We
live in a nation where provision for the infirm is left to the whims of
fortune. By the time old women reach 70, the possible burdens of the
future come into focus. Even among the wealthy (as others see them),
the possibility of living for a long time at great cost is counterbal-
anced by the fear of not living longer. Josie had an over 100-year-old
mother-in-law who lived in a residential facility for twenty years, bedridden and with additional 24-hour care at a cost of almost $150,000
a year. Josie says, "We have enough no matter how long she lives, but
what about those who don't?" This old woman eventually died at the
age of 107.

Eve has considerable assets and adult children and grandchildren
who are well taken care of financially. She wants to take cruises, and

she wants to have another face-lift, but she is afraid of running out of money as she gets older and needs care. Candy and her husband are also well off, but even with no children, she says that she worries about running out of money as she ages. She colors her own hair in order to avoid the (not inconsiderable) expense of salon procedures and says, "I am cheap" because of the threat of aging. In the absence of collective solutions to the problem of paying for the care of helpless elders, individuals and families have to come up with ad hoc solutions. For most of the old people in deteriorating health, even among the wealthy, spouses provide caregiving, with neighbors and friends assisting. Jolene says:

> I took care of Syl for more than a year before he died. We had some help through his insurance. Our friends brought us food and visited. The next-door neighbors took care of the dogs a lot.

Old people have families as well as partners and spouses. A few have very old parents who live with them or in nursing homes. Although some have no adult offspring, most have adult children and grandchildren; the oldest have great-grandchildren. Laura—together with her husband—is a part-time caregiver and babysitter for an entire network of people: four parents and stepparents hovering around the age of 90, three adult offspring and two husbands, and five grandchildren. She says: "I run around all the time, I am in and out and they are in and out. I am exhausted most of the time."

Our offspring and other relatives are among those who observe us and comment on our bodies/ourselves, either among themselves or to us directly. Viola says that her 20-year-old daughter has commented on:

> "How old I look. I have a bald spot on the top of my head. I wear the wrong shoes. I talk too loudly. My teeth need to be whitened. My new sunglasses make me look like Woody Woodpecker."

Our adult sons do not criticize our clothing or appearance; instead, they compliment us when we wear something that they approve of. Carol:

"My son Ian, when I was in my late fifties and he was going to high school, did ask me to modify my eyebrows. They were doing that whitening and thinning and bushy thing that eyebrows do. I tried to tidy them up."

Our sons gave up on trying to improve our appearances by the time we reached our sixties, except perhaps to accentuate the less negative. When Carol, in her early seventies, wore a subdued (for once) outfit of gray and beige, Kathi's son said that he liked it.

Our communities, social circles and family are set within time and space. We live in ways that have been common for thousands of years of Western culture, and we live in different parts of the United States. There are regional and local as well as cultural (those glossy magazines) ways of the aging body. In the "white wine party" New York world of Alexandra Sifferlin (2016), slim power-women in their fifties have had face-lifts and tummy tucks. In Southern California, wealthy women have had those procedures and speak of them freely. A 70-year-old woman emailed us, saying that

> When I go to the theater in Santa Monica, Calif., I am the only woman of my age with gray hair. In Cambridge, Mass., . . . I look pretty much like the rest of my age mates.

The hall of mirrors shows our public bodies to others, clothed and adorned. In the 1950s, adults, teenagers and children wore clothing that announced their age, with girls' and women' passage points marked by such adornments as lipstick, high heels, pearls and white gloves. Today, anything goes, at any age. The old women want to look stylish, they want to look slender and some of them want to look wealthy; their clothing and jewelry of choice reflects these themes. They also want to look youthful enough—but not too youthful.

> Bridget comes into the restaurant patio wearing short shorts and a tank top. It is early evening, and cocktails and appetizers are being served. "Will you look at that," murmurs Eve.

Therese, 80, is wearing a beret cocked to one side and a very short skirt over knee socks and Mary Janes. "No way," one of the observing women mutters.

Jewelry serves as a bodily distractor for the old women, as we saw in Chapter 4. It is also a status emphasizer for the old women. A sparkling five-carat diamond on a ring finger shows that the woman wearing it is, or once was, the object of male desire and possession. Expensive jewelry emphasizes the old woman's status, as wealthy in her own right or by right of her husband or husbands or partner. When complimented on a piece of jewelry, a woman gives its marital history:

Clarissa: "'My second husband gave me this (diamond bracelet) on our tenth anniversary. He bought this (gold bracelet) for me when we took a cruise in the Greek Islands."

Mindi: In response to several admiring comments about her enormous diamond wedding ring: "Yes, I had to put out for that," and with a perfectly timed comic pause, "several times."

In the hall of mirrors, the old women are embodied, adorned and reflected through the prisms of wealth and marriage. And, as we have seen throughout all these chapters, they observe and then talk about their own and each other's bodies.

We old women are in overlapping social circles, which intersect with overlapping sets of professionals who, in one way or another, work on our bodies. We talk about those providers and what they have told us. We swap recommendations for a good hair stylist or a manicurist who does not charge an arm and a leg. And we recommend—or not—those whom we entrust with our health.

Kathi: "I told Nora about the exercise that my physical therapist recommended for my shoulder. She tried it, and it worked! She called the PT and cancelled her appointment for the next day, because the PT told her that she would have shown her that exact exercise."

Carol: "The last time I saw our doctor I had looked up the protocol for taking blood pressure, and they did not do it that way. I had blood pressure over the limit. I then asked her to have my blood pressure taken the proper way. Both feet on the floor, no talking, for ten minutes. When the nurse took it again it had gone down twenty-three points, below my age limit for blood pressure medication."

Viola: "My dentist said I had to have all four front teeth veneered, at $800 each, before I could have the rest of them whitened."

Carol: "The way they did mine, they bleached all but the two front teeth and then matched the new caps to that shade. If you only need one tooth veneered they could do it that way."

A constant refrain of the old women is the cost of both routine and cosmetic dental work and the mystery surrounding procedures and costs. The dentists hold our teeth in their hands, but the doctors hold our bodies. We exchange recommendations and warnings about our doctors, from internists to cancer or heart specialists.

The hall of mirrors shows us the aging of friends and neighbors, as well as partners and parents. The 70-year-old woman who visits a couple in their early nineties sees one possible future reflected in the glass. Phyllis does not like what she sees:

Phyllis: "I spoke with Norma and her husband today."

Kathi: "How were they?"

Phyllis: "Terrible. Norma went on and on about how awful things are, they can't get out and do anything. I don't want to be like that. I don't want to live so long that there is nothing to live for."

Kathi: "Yes but you may change your mind when you are ninety!"

Phyllis says ruefully, 'I know!' and we all laugh.

We all say we don't want to live so long that we are a burden, or in terrible pain, or disabled, or without the use of our brains and senses. But when that time comes, who knows if we will continue to want to live or wish to die.

Many of the old women have parents who are still alive but have dementia, or who died in the wake of dementia—providing several dimensions of mirroring. Aging women who have mothers with dementia may experience a different kind of parent than they had when young. Viola said that

> "My mother was always critical, never kissed me or said she loved me. Once she got Alzheimer's she changed completely. Now she says she loves me all the time, when I go to visit she holds my hand."

Carol had a similar experience:

> "My mother was always cold and stern with me, at least as long as I can remember. She said she liked children only up to the age of seven. When she became demented she became nice, soft, warm."

The internet offers up many more examples of mothers becoming warmer and more caring once they are afflicted with dementia—referred to as "pleasant dementia." Since dementia is a personality trickster, though, there are other outcomes. At the end, Viola's mother thought Viola was a "nice lady" but did not recognize her as her daughter. The end for other women and men with dementia can be associated with more, not less, abusive behavior.

Old women's relationships with adult offspring inhabit their own hall of mirrors. In photographs, in dreams and in reveries we see and know our children when they were babies, toddlers, 9-year-olds, teenagers, college-bound. With each child we have at least eighteen children of memory—what J.K. Rowling calls "our little ghosts." We mourn our lost children at the same moment we celebrate our 30- or 40- or 50-year-old adult offspring. We are lucky to have them in our lives. Others do not, having lost adult offspring to estrangement or to illness or death.

Eve: "My son will not talk to me and has not talked to me for about eight years. His therapist said it would be best to cut me off. He has some kind of mental illness. I miss my granddaughter. I used to take care of her, and now I never see her."

Nora: "I have a son in his fifties who is a crack addict. My daughter died at fifty of breast cancer."

It is a truism that Americans are unfamiliar with death in everyday life, but this is not so true in some places: nursing homes and the street where we live are among them. We see sudden death, and we see decline and death. Women watch as their husbands die, either suddenly or slowly. Kay was inside her house with her husband when he dropped dead of a heart attack in the front yard. Jolene's neighbor called 911 when Syl suffered a massive heart attack:

> "They sent him home after about a month. He got an infection in his chest and had to go back to the hospital. He came back home again and he was all right for a while, but it was very difficult for me having to care for him. Then he was in and out of the hospital and rehab places for months."

Syl died in the hospital, in a coma, eighteen months after the initial heart attack.

In the hall of mirrors, others' deaths reflect our own deaths back to us. At "only" 56, Sheila Nevin "had to write a will today. Mine. Or at least revise an old boilerplate version I'd written when dying was for other people." As Nora Ephron (2003) at "only" 64 said: "Death is a sniper. It strikes people you love, people you like, people you know. It's everywhere. You could be next." The deaths of others, the deterioration of our bodies and the number of our years reflect our deaths within the hall of mirrors. In *memento mori*, "Each person has a specific fear about aging and death, so we watch as each fearful imagining comes true" (Steinem, 2006: ii).

Eve says that "I don't want to check out just yet."
Carol: "Why would you, you are perfectly healthy."
Eve: "Yes, but any moment I could have a stomachache that turns out to be pancreatic cancer. The rates of all cancers increase as you get older."

We thought about this and could not think of any examples to the contrary—except for those cancers that can no longer take root in their original sites: breast, uterine, cervical, ovarian and endometrial. Even with the loss of specific cancer sites, many more remain in play through the lifespan.

Death will come, for most of us, in its own time. But for some old women there is suicide or physician-assisted suicide. Suicide rates are not an exact measure of how many people take their own lives, because coroners make cause-of-death decisions. A coroner's choosing between homicide, suicide, natural or unexplained causes of death may be a matter of context, including the religious, political and family sensitivities of the communities where the coroners work. Suicide statistics do not mirror suicides, but they give us some idea. For example, men commit suicide more often than women, by a factor of about 3.5 (www.tps.org). The highest rate of suicide in 2015 was for men 85 years old and older. Among men 75 years old and older the suicide rate was 38.8 per 100,000 for men, and 4 per 100,000 for women (Tavernise, 2016). The suicide rate for women 75 and older had a downward trend from 1999 to 2014 (www.tps.org). But during those same years, there was a 63% increase in suicide among women aged 45 to 64.

Physician-assisted suicide is legal—as of this writing—in Oregon, Washington, Montana, Arizona and California. In order to qualify for physician-assisted suicide, patients must be terminal, mentally competent and able to afford the medical costs. Two out of three physician-assisted suicides are for those over 65, and the median age is 71. The reasons given by these patients include loss of autonomy, activity and dignity (www.deathwithdignity.com). Mandy, suffering from a fatal autoimmune condition, chose physician-assisted suicide. She wrote in an email to friends and family:

The doors swing open and the doors swing shut
The time has come to find out "what's what!"
So come say goodbye and don't be downcast
The ride's been a blast but it's over at last.

You are invited to Mandy's last hurrah. . . . Food, beverages, music and party favors will be provided . . . come prepared to share a story, tell a joke, and help Mandy celebrate "her way."

A few hours after the last guest departed, Mandy died by morphine drip, listening to a Frank Sinatra recording of "My Way," her children beside her.

Some old women worry that they do not have the means to die by their own hands, or in the hands of their doctors and families, if life is made intolerable by severe pain, looming dementia or lack of funds. In nursing homes in this country—unless otherwise specified and with watertight paperwork—old people who want to be left alone to die may be force-fed or medicated for a brief revival. The presumption is that old people's ailments—pneumonia, heart attacks—will be treated medically. This assumption is reversed in England and some European countries.

Carol: "My mother was in a residential facility in England when she died of dementia. Before she died I had to sign some forms, which I discussed with staff. They advised me to sign a form waiving medication if my mother contracted pneumonia. As someone who suffers from lung problems I could not bear the idea of anyone gasping for breath, so I did not sign. She did recover from pneumonia once before she died."

As we said in Chapter 1, there is a great distance between 60 and 90. Loe (2011), who interviewed thirty people aged between 85 and 102, says that these elders tell stories of creativity and resilience that are inspiring, but also, at times, painful" (p. 6).

Among the twenty or so women we know who are over 85, that pain often results from chronic conditions, such as Mandy's autoimmune disorder, or from accidents, such as Norma's falling after tripping over her dog. At times, several months before she died, Mandy had said that she was ready to die. This was not only because she was old and lived alone; she had a lively social group and a lively attitude. It was because of the intermittent and interminable pain consequent upon a degenerative disease. Her pain was sometimes tractable to medical marijuana or opiates, and sometimes not. At those times she said, "Today is one of those days I would like to die." And then she did.

As we said at the beginning of the book, 70 is not the new 60. Nor is 90 the new 80. The challenges we face now are not the same as the ones we will face, if we live to face them, at 90. All we can do is make a pact, between ourselves, among the old women, and with our readers. If and when we reach the borderlands of very old age, we will write again, looking back into, and from, the hall of mirrors. In the meantime, we face the future with resilience, shaped by circumstances, social networks—and luck. Our refrain is: "Aging sucks"—the chorus is, "But it's better than the alternative"—and our bodies are still ourselves.

7
EPILOGUE
Our Bodies Ourselves

The paradox of old age is that our bodies are not ourselves and yet they are ourselves—we have nothing else; we are embodied. Facing decline, disability, illness and death, our aging bodies come less and less to resemble the selves we luxuriated in in our youth. But our aging bodies are ourselves, because in the here and now they are all we have, and we are forced to adapt. So we cope, in the context of resilience, privilege and stable social networks, feeling much luckier than those who are not resilient, privileged or loved. We laugh. We fend off invisibility and fight to be heard. We plan for the future and revisit the past in mourning or in joy. We think about minds or souls, wondering if there are reincarnations or lives after death. And, still, sometimes we enjoy ourselves within the world, and we come to terms with our bodies as ourselves, for that moment in time and place.

Many of the old women in this book have been resilient throughout their lifetimes, overcoming the death of children or grandchildren, breast cancer, heart attacks and the loss of a spouse. This resilience continues into old age, in the context of circumstances and social circles. Our circumstances, we old women, are ideal for the drawing-together of strength and social support in old age. We are privileged, with enough (to considerable) resources and medical care. Those of us living in Southern California do not have to worry about frozen water pipes or who is going to remove snow from the driveway. We can take walks and visit one another without precautions and problems, for as long as we can. Those of us living in the Midwest, embedded in extended families, take comfort from our children and grandchildren. Old women in cultural centers enjoy the theater and fine dining. In these and other geographical and social contexts, we try to live so that aging is better than the alternative, each in her own way and from moment to moment.

In the present, we engage with family and friends and with a world of strangers; in that way, we can reclaim our bodies within the social network. Families and social networks protect against the loneliness of old age. Most of the old women that we know are embedded in social networks that support them in health as well as in sickness. And most have families. Laura and her husband spend most of their time in activities supportive of their children, grandchildren, parents and siblings, driving from one end of the country to the other to attend graduations, weddings and childbirth. Esther and many of the women are "granny nannies" to their grandchildren in nearby communities. Nora is single, but "I am busy all the time." Some women in their seventies are taking care of parents in their nineties and upward.

For those old women who are in pleasing partnerships or marriages, the household is a place of comfort and enjoyment. Although illness may be depressing and caregiving stressful, the nurturing that flows between the couple is its own form of nourishment. There may be other people in the household who can offer support, and there are pets to provide interest, companionship and touch. Ruby says of her dog Toto: "He loves me. But he and my husband are really bonded, they enjoy each other. And Toto provides all kinds of engagement between us, we are less likely to feel bored." Cats and dogs in particular can be as dangerous to old people as throw rugs, but their loving touch and attention are dear to many of us.

Both our households and our social circles provide us with information about our bodies. Couples and friends routinely share what each other has learned from doctors, dentists, physical therapists and other informational sources, such as the use of an extra pillow to stop snoring. Expert and lay advice becomes part of the wider informational grid of growing old. Carol was walking with her cane and encountered the

93-year-old father of a neighbor who told her: "My doctor said never to walk with one stick, always with two, because walking with one stick can contribute to problems with your hip or knee."

Our social circles also promote pleasurable bodily activities. The sorrow of no longer being able to play tennis is muted by play golfing with a new friend; the sadness of no longer being able to play golf gives way to a gentle walking pace, greeting acquaintances along the way. Our neighborhood institutions—from yacht clubs to churches—organize parties and other events that enable us to enjoy what is around us, whether ocean, mountains or cityscapes. For those who cannot get out and about, either temporarily or permanently, the computer offers contact and companionship: keeping up with grandchildren, watching sitcoms, Facebook, Words with Friends; whatever worlds await the old woman. The inhabitants of the hall of mirrors show us that we are old, reflect the illnesses, deterioration and deaths of our friends, and remind us of lost youth and things past. But they also show us hope.

> We are planning various stops on our road trip. We are going to have lunch with a couple in their early nineties who live in the Bay Area. They say that 12:30 or 1:00 would be a better time for them than noon. We think, oh dear, they must be very slow getting up and getting going. But Bella writes: "Jack will be playing tennis earlier, and I will be at the gym, so we won't be back home until noon."

Couples and friends socialize, plan, work together and, above all, laugh together, at jokes, at the vicissitudes of everyday life, at our own foibles and those of our friends. We laugh with people who are younger than we are, people who are older and people who are the same age; we laugh in restaurants, clubs and bars, at dinner parties, on boats and trains. Wherever we can be together, we laugh. What our laughter is about is not easily shared; we laugh, it seems, at everything and nothing. It is impossible to tell what the laughing is all about, because it depends upon the context, the moment and the mood And laughter is not just sound, it is a whole-body experience. When we laugh, our facial muscles, breath and nervous system are involved. And for the old people, there is old age humor, shared by us in households and among friends and family—on the phone, on the internet and in the exchange of greeting cards.

Shared humor between friends and partners takes the mordant aspects of aging and shares them as funny rather than disconcerting or frightening. Everything is mocked: memory loss, shrinking skeletons, golf scores, wrinkles, gray hair. Men and women make fun of their aging bodies and make us laugh. At a bocce ball tournament, sixtyish Janine was wearing a skimpy halter top that revealed a large amount of cleavage every time she leaned forward to throw the ball. James was sitting next to us; he had gained quite a bit of belly and weight since we last saw him. Watching Janine, he said, "I used to like big boobs until I grew them." Humor in the face of aging bodies permeates our social groups and follows us into households and their electronic extensions.

In the household:

Kathi: "It was kind of frightening this morning when the garage door opener was right in front of me in the drawer, and I had looked for it twice."
Carol: "At least it was in the drawer, not in the freezer!"
We are watching a TV program. Kathi says something that Carol hears as the "Chameleon Conservation Corps." No, she says, it is the "Civilian Conservation Corps." We laugh away the threat of continued hearing loss.

On the phone:

Louise is having back surgery. She asks about SueAnn, who had the same back surgery and is recovering.
Carol: "Well, they thought it was her back but it was actually her gall bladder."
Louise: "What kind of doctor confuses a bad back with a gall bladder?"
By this time we are laughing hysterically.
Carol: "I read in the *New York Times* that the third leading cause of death in this country is medical error." [What have I said?] Louise,

who is about to have surgery, laughs so much I think she is going to pass out.

In social situations:

Clarice: "I am still taking chemo drugs for my breast cancer surgery five years ago . . . now I have a lump in my throat. I am going to have a scan next week. Here, feel it."
(Kathi feels the lump, just under Clarice's chin.)
Carol: "Where does breast cancer most likely recur?"
Kathi: "In the brain, I think."
Clarice: "Well, I suppose my brain has moved." (much laughter)

Humor and laughter flourish even when death is literally knocking on the door. Zelda and Simon, both in their late eighties, lived at home, resisting the attempts of their offspring to place them in a nursing home. Hospice was brought in for Zelda, who was bedridden and given morphine. Their son Saul and a friend, Josie, gathered by Zelda's bedside, with Simon in a wheelchair beside her.

Zelda complained that the room smelled bad.
Josie: "Why?" Zelda replied "Well, there is a fish under my bed."
Saul: "What color is it?"
Zelda: "Black."
Josie: "How did get in?"
Zelda: "It flew in through the window!"

By this time, everyone in the room, including Zelda, was convulsed with laughter.

And then there is the internet. The internet is a fountainhead of old age humor, both between people who know each other and among strangers who do not know each other but who share the experience of aging. The exchange of old age humor through emails is ubiquitous among the old women and men, both text and images. Ruby's 87-year-old brother sent her an internet old-person joke that includes the lines:

"Sometimes I'm in Capable and I go there more often as
I'm getting old . . .
I may have been in Continent, but I don't remember."

Wilma sends out on email, "When is this 'Old Enough to Know Better'
supposed to kick in?"

Birthdays mark time and age, from the first to the last. We send out
birthday cards, either on paper or via the internet. Some birthday cards
mark specific ages (up to 100)—and don't appear to be very humorous—
while others mock aging. By 70, we had begun to send out age-mocking
cards, mainly to those who had sent them to us. Some cards are designed
to be sent to anyone, others to men or women. Making fun of men who
are going deaf:

The birthday card shows three men on a golf course.
The man on the left says: "It's a nice day"
The man in the middle says: "No it's Thursday not Wednesday"
The man on the right says: "I don't think it's a holiday."

Making fun of women who are experiencing memory loss:

Two white-haired women are in the front seat of a convertible,
scenery streaming past. The woman on the left says:
"Where are we going?"
The woman on the right says: "I thought you were driving."

There is somewhat of a delicate dance to be performed here between
humor and insult. The sender may be more inclined to send such cards
to people who have already sent them, or to men rather than women,
or vice versa. We have sent a similar golf course card to a man for his
seventieth birthday, but only because he is NOT hard of hearing—or
have anything else wrong with his body, for that matter. We have sent
a similar card to a woman for her seventy-fifth, but one who is still
working in a professional position and with no memory problems. Both
these people had previously sent us slightly "age insulting" cards.

One of this book's reviewers suggested that the inclusion of old age humor in our narrative is "ageist." Going even further, one gerontologist claims that "Humour is the last refuge of hate speech" (Gullette 2015: 23). Ylanne (2015: 374), who studied British television advertisements in the 2000s, found that although some old age humor was "Cheeky, fun or playful," other, more ageist advertisements were "denigratory" or "mocking," ridiculing old people as grumpy, out of it or repulsive. We old people do not want to be presented in these ways, even if our behavior sometimes warrants it. But we reserve the right to use old-age humor among ourselves, as we face our gradual invisibility and the deterioration of our senses. Just as the racist "n" word is appropriated by African-Americans in song lyrics and conversations, we old people appropriate old age humor.

When we are with our friends and family, we are visible. But when we are out in the world among strangers—from store clerks to passers-by—we old women are invisible. For women, the process of aging is also a process of disappearance. As Hess (2017) says, women's visibility is in the eyes of others, and "we spend our lives fighting our own disappearance." Old men also feel invisible; as Jacob says, at 75, "I have the red sports car because I don't want to be invisible. I may be invisible, but people can see the car." We can and do shrink into the background everywhere and anywhere. On the other hand, as Twigg and Martin (2015: 5) remark, an old woman is also "hypervisible" in the sense that her old age is the only thing that is seen by the observer.

Hypervisibility is one source of the ageist infantilization of old women, often in public and on the part of service providers: grocery store clerks, bus drivers or hospital workers (who could and should be better trained). What old woman is not used to—but still annoyed by—the grocery clerk who calls her "Honey" or "Dear"; as Leland (2018) notes, these "terms of endearment are really terms of condescension." These terms of condescension are said both to and about the old woman. Leland says of the daughter of one of his "oldest old" respondents:

> She would be out with her mother and someone would say, 'Oh your mother is cute!" And she would say, "My mother is not cute!"
> (Reporter, www.www.NPR.org, Jan 25 2018)

There are other public behaviors that are infantilizing, including call-ing old people by their first names and offering help. Although generally comfortable with the informality of California's folkways, we cringe at being called "Kathi" or "Carol" by strangers a quarter of our age. We do not mind offers of help in carrying things, although other old women do. Gloria, who is 70, complains that her daughter offers to hold her arm when she crosses the road and tells her to be "careful." Mary, 74, who lives in the country, says:

> I totally resent and get almost violent when I am addressed as: "honey, sweetie, dear, sweetheart" Many times this is followed by: "do you need some help carrying that out?" What the hell? If they help me carry out my 5 bags of groceries, who do they think will carry them into my house? Some times if I am really fed up, I ask if they would like to come home with me and carry the bags into my house? This tends to shut them up.

> I am not their "sweetie" so, you get my drift? If my husband is with me and this happens, I see fear in his eyes, he is just hoping I don't go off !! Some times, I must admit, I do correct the sweet little clerk . . .

> I love the feed store, when I have two 40 lb bags of bird seed, two sacks of dog food, etc. they just figure if I bought it, I can carry it and slam it into the bed of my truck.

If the old women do not want to be invisible out in the world, they must adorn and display their bodies in ways that it would be impossible not to notice. Iris Apfel, born in 1921, is famous for her being-in-the-world (Givhan, 2015). She is hypervisible in a different way—the observer cannot miss seeing her. She

> looks like a cross between a peacock and an owl. She has a plume of white hair, a slender physique, and above-average height. She typically wears a pair of round black-framed glasses that have the

circumference of a saucer. She dresses in colorful clothes that are made up of everything from designer trousers to ecclesiastical robes, accessorized with layers of thick bracelets and necklaces.

Although Iris wears little makeup and has had no cosmetic surgery, she is tall, with an "upright carriage." Iris will not be invisible as an individual, no matter what.

Some of the women in their seventies and eighties that we know have a presentation of self which makes them more visible than we others. Kitty, for example, has hair that is short and silver, spiked at the crown. She wears low-cut tops that show a lot of cleavage and colorful, draped clothes. Her ears are adorned with rows of earrings. Eve is tall, straight, slender and regal and will be noticed in any room. But most of us look relatively ordinary as we go about in the world. Marlene says, "What is hard about being old is that you are not there for other people." Carol says: "You could dye your hair blue and then you would be noticed." Marlene: "But then people would think I'm crazy." The choices of appearance for old women: invisible or crazy.

As we saw in Chapter 1, the Western narratives of old age represent we old people as at least partially to blame for our invisibility. We have been described, since ancient times, as crabbed, disapproving, grouchy and with downcast mouth and eyes, passing by the youthful without a glance. Or, worse, moaning and complaining about the running-around of children or the fixation of teenagers upon their screens—making ourselves visible, but not in a good way. We think there is some truth to this; we both have less patience, over time, with the ways in which we perceive younger people acting in public—less polite, more pushy, driving madly. We were with friends in a restaurant not too long ago; at the next table there was a family with three children aged about 2, 5 and 9. They were somewhat noisy and somewhat mobile. The four of us were somewhat to greatly annoyed by these children, but there were no other tables available to move to.

But being invisible or patronized on the one hand or critical and grouchy on the other is not always the case; there are unexpected and pleasant moments of connection between old women and strangers, bright spots in the continuum of (in)visibility in the swirl of every-day life:

> We are checking out our groceries. The checker is a tall young man with dark hair. He looks and smiles at us as he is ringing the items up: "You have a lot of good stuff there." Carol: "How much do we think we have?" Kathi: "A hundred and forty-three dol-lars." Carol: "A hundred and sixty dollars." To the checker: "How much would you guess?" Kathi: "You are the one most likely to be right!" He was not right; we all laughed as we left.

There was smiling in this exchange, and laughter: a momentary visibility between strangers, old and young.

We may or may not be invisible to strangers, depending upon our demeanor or style, but we are visible to our family and friends (in per-son, on the internet, on FaceTime or Skype). Mostly, as we saw in the last chapters, they take our bodies and ourselves just as we are. What we want from family members is to be heard by them—not ignored. When we feel unheard by our family members, we feel unvalued. Ruby says of her son: "I have so much wisdom to give, and so much information to give also. He is buying commercial property, and I know a lot about it. But he does not ask. I wish he would ask." Annette says,

> "My daughter insisted that she could carry on three bags when she was flying back home. She would not listen to me when I told her it was only two. So she had to check one bag, and then it got lost."

We want our son and daughter to hear our longing for a phone call or a visit—although, of course, we do not want to pantomime the bathos of the clinging, demanding mother-as-martyr.

Among our friends we old women are always heard, because mutual hearing is part of the flow of friendship. For those of us in good part-nerships and marriages, hearing one another—while we can both still hear—provides yet another layer of comfort between our day to day aging bodies and ourselves. And being seen and heard is enhanced, as Rees Jones (2015) demonstrates, by the possibilities inherent in information and communication technologies (ICTs). We met an 80-year-old woman in New Zealand—"Mum"—who, when she moved from the UK as a new bride, did not see or speak to her mother for twenty-five years. Letters were the only form of communication. Today, old people can keep in touch with their children and grandchildren, seeing and speaking to them, with several of the ICTs or, perhaps, reconnect with an old love.

For humans, time is sensed as past and future as well as present, so that we have autobiographies and we have plans. The past is a mixed bag for the old women. The melancholia of old age is sometimes brought on by experiencing the past-in-present, by reminiscences of past times. A poet in her late sixties, looking at "Friends' Photos" in old albums, is nostalgic for past beauty and lost glamour (Segal, 2013: 187). But remembering things past can also bring solace. Carol: "'Showing my son's fiancée photos of my son when he was a baby, a toddler, an eight year old, a high schooler playing the clarinet, I remembered those times with great joy." Remembered moments of pleasure are set against the loss, fear and melancholia of old age. In a poem "The Little Old Lady in Lavender Silk," Dorothy Parker, who died in 1967, fuses memory and humor as she confronts old age. Claiming that at 77 she has not yet lost but "will shortly be losing my bloom," she says of old age and sex that " there was nothing more fun than a man," that she has no regrets, and that she would do it all over again if she could (Parker, 1988: 20). Several of the old widows look back at their marriages and sex lives with sadness for what they lost but also with great joy for what they had.

Framing the future is one way in which we hold on to the possibility of its existence. We old women make plans, and we learn new things. Nora plans to travel to Egypt next year and an African safari the next. She also wants "to learn to play the piano just like Beethoven." Mandy, before she died, started an internet business, hoping to sell the jewelry and knitted items that she made as a hobby. Rosie takes classes for seniors at her local college and belongs to several book clubs. Kathi is learning Spanish and tackling more and more difficult pieces on the piano and ukulele; Kathi and Carol are planning a cruise for Carol's seventy-fifth birthday.

The future is also present in the form of adult children, grandchildren and great-grandchildren. Musing on her recent knee surgery and aging body, Rosie writes:

> Marriages, births, new beginnings—it helps me put our own personal declines into perspective . . . the knee replacement was very easy . . . but all the former pain hopped over to the other side of my body. . . . Isn't this boring talking about this? But how can we not? It's reality now, it's really happening to us, and we have to deal with it. Anyway, life is also good and we're enjoying good weather and lots of great visits from family and friends.

Like Rosie, the old women purposely wrench their thoughts from bodily aging into other, more positive subjects.

While autobiographical—lost, or to be found—the past and the future are fused, at times, with the present; in the contemplation of objects, in activities and in the habits of the heart. There is a considerable literature on the significance of objects—our "things"—in the lives of old women. Our things ground us in our present environment and activities and in their past acquisition. One of the deep sorrows of moving from one's home into a retirement home is the culling of things, which is in a sense the culling of self (Ekerdt, 2015). We surround ourselves with photographs of good people and good times; with mementos of travel; with art that pleases us; with cooking pots that have made our recipes. Glancing upon and using objects melds past and present into a sense of comfortable familiarity. We hope to stay in our homes, among our things and memories, forever—or as long as we can.

In our home, there are paintings and drawings by Esther, who moved away but has since returned, and by Alice, who lives nearby. The curvy stainless steel and blue neon CD holder—and no more need for CDs. Kathi's old butcher block desk with chrome legs, now a kitchen dining table. A large piece of lapis lazuli from Carol's son's deployment to Afghanistan. The 30-year-old dining room set saved from Carol's divorce settlement and reupholstered by Kathi. A reproduction of an ancient Roman plaque from our trip to Bath twenty years ago. A cut-glass vase that was one of Kathi's wedding presents from the 1980s. Each room contains whole lives of memories.

When Carol was much younger, her father told her how important it is for old people to have routines. At the time she rolled her eyes; now she is in agreement. Having routines for the days, weeks and months, for the household, for interaction with others, provides several kinds of reassurance. We do not have to wonder what we are supposed to be doing next, or where we are, or why we are where we are. Mornings are for coffee and the *New York Times* and watching the sunrise over our beautiful San Diego Bay. Tuesday is discount day at our favorite store. In November there are lots of birthdays and Thanksgiving, Kathi's favorite holiday. Our household routines are designed to foil any memory deficits we might be developing. The car keys go in a particular corner of a particular drawer in the kitchen. The cell phone is put on the hall table.

For some old people, it is the non-routine that provides a sense of purpose. Robert Goldfarb (www.nyt.com: 2018) is 88 and has been married "since Eisenhower was elected President." He recently decided to "find my younger self" by varying some of their everyday routines (he does not say what his wife thought of the new arrangement). Instead of going to their usual restaurants or watching their usual TV programs, "spontaneously, one of us will suggest going to a coffee shop or café just to talk, and we do." Several readers commented favorably on Goldfarb's essay, and some had additional suggestions for varying routines or staying close to their "younger selves."

Breaks in routine may be delightful but must be calibrated carefully to the aging individual—routine punctuated by the non-routine. For the Goldfarbs, it is a trip to the coffee shop. For us, it is a cruise that goes in and out of San Diego, our home port. In our fifties and sixties, we took frequent trips to Europe without much in the way of consequences. But now, in our seventies, they represent a disruption of our routines that disturbs sleep for days or weeks. The toll of jet lag, and even the onset of Daylight Saving Time in the spring and the return to Standard Time in the fall, seems to take a toll on our bodies and minds. For us, at the moment, both routines and their (pleasant) interruption are part of the comforts of growing old. Others are different. Ruby says she would still happily travel to Europe if her husband were well enough to accompany her. And we know two couples in their nineties who take frequent plane, train or cruise trips.

Our activities and roles change as we age, along with our relationships. As a young married woman, Eve did a lot of cooking. With her third husband, she says, "We eat out most of the time. I am done cooking." Annette loved the beach:

> When I was in my twenties I did a lot of body surfing. In my thirties I started boogie boarding instead. I still do it once or twice a year. Thinking back to the energy I had then, and how golden the days seemed. I can be sad for those past days. But then I can say, "I rode six waves today." And: "same time next year."

As she says, for the old women it is important to focus on the enjoyment of the day and the promise of next year rather than the days that are no more.

We have seen, in earlier chapters, the meaning of body and motion to the old women. For some, their essential selves seemed to dwell in their faces, which once were beautiful and unlined; now, they might still be beautiful, but lines groove their cheeks. For others, the athletes, the centrality of their body's strength and motion eases into a gentler routine: the shortened golf swing for stiff shoulders, the adjusted tennis serve. For those women whose lives revolved around cooking and cleaning for their families, the soreness of their arthritic hands and the distances between themselves and their children renders the thought of family gatherings melancholy. But we are still alive.

But, sooner or later, we will die. Western and Eastern cultures have various ways of denying the finality of death. Dylan Thomas draws upon the theme of transcending death in his glorious poem "And Death Shall Have No Dominion"—but of course, death does have its dominion, something that cultures have explored since the beginning of time. Ways of thinking about—and doing something about—the fatedness of death are part of

Western culture. In our contemporary world, science and technology hold out the promise of extending the lifespan and staving off death. Cryogenics—the freezing of the body for possible future revival—and the cloning of the flesh are among our options, although thus far cloning has been limited to our pets and not ourselves. These technologies hold out hope for those whose approach to death is denial. La Perla (2018: 81) says that those of the old people who are baby boomers are

> resistant to the outing of death. "Their idea is to give death the slip. . . . I'm eating well. I'm exercising. I can do things to my face. . . . I'll survive."

The old women can draw upon religious or spiritual beliefs to deny the finality of death. The aging body is framed as a shell that, when cast off, moves into another realm or state. Gloria Vanderbilt, at 91, toys with the possibility of reincarnation (Cooper and Vanderbilt, 2016), something more common in Eastern than Judeo-Christian faiths. Christian religions offer a belief in the afterlife. At a dinner party with six people ranging in age from 70 to 81, two people spoke about their dying parents:

Eve: "My mother was in a coma and had been lying in bed flat on her back for months. We were sitting by her, and suddenly she sat up and said 'John. I am not quite ready yet. I will come when I am ready.' She lay back down and died a few weeks later. "

Keith told an almost identical story about his mother sitting up and saying hello to her long-dead husband. Both Keith and Eve and their respective spouses interpreted these events as a message from their parents that the afterlife is real and that they will join their loved ones there. Sylvia believed that she—and her dogs, but possibly not her husband—would go to a heaven in which

> "there are doors for Presbyterians, Catholics, Baptists, and so on, I will go through the door marked 'Episcopalian.' Carol: "Are there doors for Muslims, Jews, Hindus?" Sylvia: "Well . . . no."

Nonreligious old people may describe themselves as "spiritual," referring to a belief in something that transcends the material world and the embodied self. Spiritualists propose the possibility of an afterlife of ghosts or spirits, lingering in the earthly realms where they lived and died. Wanda describes the death of her mother, who was in her late sixties:

"She had a lot of friends—spiritualists, astrologers—I don't believe in any of it. We were all sitting around after she died talking about her. A bird flew into the house, and went into every room, and then flew out. Her friends were all in agreement that this was my mother."

Other old people take rational approaches to death, assessing and planning for it as for any other event. Ruby says that her husband will not talk about anything relating to death, so she talks with us. She attended a day-long seminar of the Hemlock Society, an organization that promotes the right to die by one's own or assisted suicide and provides information to that end. Ruby also bought an app for her phone called WeCroak, which reminds users five times a day that they are going to die. WeCroak, in 2018, was one of the most popular paid health and fitness apps from the App store and appealed mostly to young people (La Perla, 2018: 81). Ruby did not like WeCroak because its sayings were "not good enough," an evaluation shared by other users. For our part, we think that this saying from the WeCroak app would give us pause:

The graves are full of ruined bones, of speechless death-rattles.
Pablo Neruda

(La Perla, 2018: 81).

Another softening of the approach of death is the idea of humankind as a whole, of which the individual is only one part. Mitteldorf and Sagan (2016) "recognize that individual lives do not belong to us alone but to our species" (p. 296). This way of seeing life and death is probably more comforting to those who have children and grandchildren of at least the prospect of grandchildren, finding comfort in "the persistence of our good works . . . [and] family legacy." Inventors, writers, artists or recorded musicians may see aspects of themselves as markers of immortality, or at least the future. But still, the body ages as it moves toward the end and must be dealt with day in, day out, until that moment comes.

The resilience of the old women ensures that they will do what they can, when they can, with their bodies in private, in public, and with others. Although old women who do not have a partner are statistically less likely to find one than old men, we know quite a few who have. Alice married in her late sixties; Eve in her late seventies. In his study of the oldest old, Leland (2018) introduces us to Helen, 90, who is in the sixth year of a relationship with a fellow nursing home resident:

> "I love Howie" she said . . . he was in a wheelchair at the side of her bed. "Same goes for me," said Howie. "You're the woman in my lifetime, I mean it." "I can't hear you," she said, "But it better be good!"

Some old women and men who have given up bodily activities resume them. Ruby's husband resumed playing tennis after several accidents and a bout with cancer; she said, "We are both delighted by this." Norma, told at 90 that she would never walk again, walked into a party in her honor and stood straight-backed for much of the ceremony. She went from her home to assisted living but then, after her husband's death, bought a new home in her old neighborhood. The 100-year-old woman can no longer walk for more than a few feet, but she enjoys being pushed around the neighborhood in her wheelchair, smiling and nodding at friends and acquaintances.

For some women, maintaining the semblance of facial as well as bodily youth is a hallmark of their old age. LouAnn, Nora and Eve continue to have cosmetic facial and other procedures as they move through their eighties, tall, slender and regal. At a dinner party, Eve describes in detail a recent procedure that involved injecting fat into her lips, eyebrows and cheeks and removing it from under her eyes. Keith looked at her from across the table and said, "You look beautiful. It was well worth it. I can see the difference." Susan has had many facial and bodily procedures. We ask her why. She says, "I want to see someone youthful in the mirror." We ask, "It is not for your husband or for anyone else?" Susan: "No, it is just for me." These women look in the mirror and see, still, the semblance of their youthful selves, blurred but brave.

And finally, the aging body can bring us unexpected delight from time to time and from moment to moment, among friends and family, with partners or by ourselves. Jean, 101 years old, when she first met Leland (2018), yelled at him: "Get me a gin!" Zelda and her friends and family laughed so hard about the fish under the bed that they cried. Eve tells us: "We went dancing on Friday. I was wearing high heels and a short, pleated skirt. I felt like a million dollars"—the music, the movement, the lights, her husband close. Closeness, deepened by the years, renders the touch of a hand on our hair poignant beyond words. We wake up in the morning after a good night's sleep, with no pain anywhere, and look out at the blue sky. We enjoy a perfect hamburger, medium rare. Out on a sailboat, we feel the wind and smell the ocean. On the beach, we walk barefoot on the warm sand and let the waves roll over our toes. We embrace those whom we most love and let the world fall away.

Our Old Bodies, Ourselves.

REFERENCES

Agosin, Marjorie, [1984] 1994. "My Belly." Pp. 329–330 in *The Oxford Book of Aging*. Eds. Thomas R. Cole and Mary G. Winkler. New York: Oxford University Press.

American Foundation for Suicide Prevention, 2015. "Suicide Statistics." https://afsp.org/about-suicide/suicide-statistics

American Society for Aesthetic Plastic Surgery, 2016. www.surgery.org

American Society of Plastic Surgeons, 2016. www.plasticsurgery.org

Bacon, Francis, [1638] 1994. "The Difference of Youth and Age." Pp. 34–35 in *The Oxford Book of Aging*. Eds. Thomas R. Cole and Mary G. Winkler. New York: Oxford University Press.

Bacon, Roger, [c1240] 1653. *The Cure of Old Age and Preservation of Health*. Trans. Richard Browne. No Publication Information.

Bassill, Nazem, 2011, March. "How Anxiety Presents Difficulty in Older Adults." www.researchgate.net

"Beautiful Old People," 2015. www.pinterest.com

Bennet, Ronni, 2012, July 18. "Old Farts: Literally." www.timegoesby.net

Bering, Jesse, 2013, July 30. "(Ever)Lasting Beauty: A Sexual Attraction to the Elderly." blogs.scientificamerican.com

Berenson, Bernard, 1994. "Body/Spirit." P. 333 in *The Oxford Book of Aging*. Eds. Thomas R Cole and Mary G. Winkler. New York: Oxford University Press.

Bordo, Susan, 1993. *Unbearable Weight: Feminism, Western Culture, and the Body*. Berkeley: University of California Press.

———, 2003. "The Empire of Images in Our World of Bodies." *The Chronicle of Higher Education* Vol. 50: pp. 1–7.

Boston Women's Health Book Collective, 2005. *Our Bodies, Ourselves: A New Edition for a New Era*. New York: Touchstone.

Brody, Jane, 2016, May 19. "Dehydration: Risks and Myths." well.blogs.nytimes.com

Brooks, Abigail, 2017. *The Ways Women Age: Using and Refusing Cosmetic Intervention*. New York: New York University Press.

Calasanti, Toni and Neal King, 2015. "Intersectionality and Age." Pp. 193–200 in *Routledge Handbook of Cultural Gerontology*. Eds Julia Twigg and Wendy Martin. New York: Routledge.

Clark, Laura Hurd, 2010. *Facing Age: Women Growing Older in American Culture*. Lanham, MD: Rowman and Littlefield.

Clark, Laura Hurd and Erica V. Bennett, 2015. "Gender, Ageing and Appearance." Pp. 133–140 in *Routledge Handbook of Cultural Gerontology*. Eds Julia Twigg and Wendy Martin. New York: Routledge.

Cooper, Anderson and Gloria Vanderbilt, 2016. *The Rainbow Comes and Goes: A Mother and Son on Life, Love, and Loss*. New York: HarperCollins.

Cohausen, J.D., 1771. *Hermippus Redivivus*. 3d ed. London.

Crichton, Sarah, 2016. "The Coming of Age." Pp. 93–103 in *The Bitch is Back*. Ed. Cathi Hanauer. New York: HarperCollins.

Crockett, Zachary, 2015, April 9. "The Science of Smelling Old." www.priceonomics.com

Death with Dignity. www.deathwithdignity.com

de Beauvoir, Simone, 1972. *The Coming of Age*. Trans. Patrick O'Brian. New York: G.P. Putnam's Sons.

Demaitre, Luke, 1990. "The Care and Extension of Old Age in Medieval Medicine." Pp. 3–22 in *Aging and the Aging in Medieval Europe*. Ed. Michael M. Sheehan. Toronto, Canada: Pontifical Institute of Medieval Studies.

Easton, James, 1799. *Human Longevity*. Salisbury: James Easton.

Ekerdt, David J., 2015. "Possessions as a Material Convoy." Pp. 313–320 in *Routledge Handbook of Cultural Gerontology*. Eds Julia Twigg and Wendy Martin. New York: Routledge.

Embarrasing Questions. https://embarrassingquestions.com

Emerson, Robert M., 2015. *Everyday Troubles: The Micro-Politics of Interpersonal Conflict*. Chicago: University of Chicago Press.

Ephron, Nora, 2006. *I Feel Bad about My Neck and Other Thoughts on Being a Woman*. New York: Knopf.

Faulkner-Wiley, India, 2001. "Laura Was Killed by Anorexia: She Was 80." www.theguardian.com

Franklin, Benjamin, 1745. "Advice to a Young Man on Taking a Mistress."

Freeman, Joseph T., 1979. *Aging: Its History and Literature*. New York: Human Sciences Press.

Friedan, Betty, 1993. *The Fountain of Age*. New York: Simon and Schuster.

Friedland, Roger, 2011, June 13. "Looking through the Bushes: The Disappearance of Pubic Hair." www.huffingtonpost.com

Fusion. www.fusion.com

Givhan, Robin, 2015, May 15. "Iris Apfel, 93 Year Old Fashion Icon, Thinks You Don't Really Know How to Shop." www.washingtonpost.com

Greer, Germaine, 1992. *The Change: Women, Aging and the Menopause*. New York: Alfred A. Knopf.

Gullette, Margaret Morganroth, 2015. "Aged by Culture." Pp. 21–36 in *Routledge Handbook of Cultural Gerontology*. Eds Julia Twigg and Wendy Martin. New York: Routledge.

Gunter, Jen, 2017, November 16. "My Vagina is Terrific. Your Opinion About It Is Not." www.newyorktimes.com

Hess, Amanda, 2014, March 3. "It's Horrible to Be an Old Woman in Hollywood, Kim Novak Edition." www.slate.com

———, 2017, September 12. "The Ever-Changing Business of 'Anti-Aging.'" www.newyorktimes.com

Holstein, Martha, 2015. *Women in Late Life: Critical Perspectives on Gender and Age*. New York: Rowman and Littlefield.

Horrocks, Sue, Maggie Somerset, Helen Stoddart and Tim J. Peters, 2004. "What Prevents Old People from Seeking Treatment for Urinary Incontinence?" *Family Practice* Vol. 21: pp. 689–696.

"Kim Novak Takes on Oscar Night Bullies in Facebook Post," 2014, April 15. www.people.com

Kleinfield, N.R., 2016, May 1. "Fraying at the Edges." *New York Times* Vol. 165, No. 57, 219. Special Section: pp. 1–11.

Kneeland, Timothy and Carol A. B. Warren, 2009. *Pushbutton Psychiatry: A Cultural History of Electroconvulsive Therapy in America*. Walnut Creek, CA: Left Coast Press.

Kontos, Pia, 2015. "Dementia and Embodiment." Pp. 181–188 in *Routledge Handbook of Cultural Gerontology*. Eds. Julia Twigg and Wendy Martin. New York: Routledge.

Kotarba, Joseph A., 1983. *Chronic Pain: Its Social Dimensions*. Thousand Oaks, CA: Sage Publications.

Kreamer, Anne, 2007. *Going Grey: What I Learned about Beauty, Sex, Work, Motherhood, Authenticity and Everything Else That Really Matters*. New York: Little Brown and Co.

La Perla, Ruth, 2018, January 14. "Think You'll Live Forever? This App Dashes All Hope." *The New York Times* Vol. 167, No. 57, 824: p. 81.

Leland, John, 2018. *Happiness Is a Choice You Make: Lessons from a Year among the Oldest Old* [Kindle Book]. Retrieved from Amazon.com

Lessius, Leonard, 1743. *Treatise on Health and Log Life*. London: Charles Hitch.

Loe, Meika, 2011. *Aging Our Way: Independent Elders, Interdependent Lives*. New York: Oxford University Press.

London South Bank Goes Geriatric? 2018. https://ageingageismdiary.wordpress.com

Martin, Wednesday, 2015. *Primates of Park Avenue: A Memoir*. New York: Simon and Schuster.

Marzorati, Gerald, 2016, May1. "Practicing for a Better Old Age." *New York Times* Vol. 165, No. 57, 219. Sunday Review: pp. 1 and 4.

Maximianus [c.550 CE], 1988. *Elegies on Old Age and Love*. Trans. R.L. Lind. Philadelphia: American Philosophical Society.

Minois, Georges, 1989. *History of Old Age: From Antiquity to the Renaissance*. Chicago: University of Chicago Press.

Mitteldorf, John and Dorion Sagan, 2016. *Cracking the Aging Code*. New York: Flatiron Books.

Myerhoff, Barbara, 1979. *Number Our Days: Triumphs of Community and Culture among Jewish People in an Urban Ghetto*. New York: Simon and Schuster.

Nevins, Sheila, 2017. *You Don't Look Your Age . . . and Other Fairy Tales*. New York: Flatiron Books.

Olds, Sharon, 2016. *Odes*. New York: Alfred A. Knopf.

Pappas, Stephanie, 2011, June 12. "Magazines' Youthful Ideal Threatens Real Women's Sexuality." www.livescience.com

Park, Michael Y., 2014, March 14. "How Our Sense of Taste Changes as We Age." www.bonappetit.com

Parker, Dorothy, 1988. "The Little Old Lady in Lavender Silk." Pp. 20–21 in *One Hundred and One Classic Love Poems*. Chicago: Contemporary Books.

Piepenbring, Dan, 2014, March 20. "Ovid's Ancient Beauty Elixirs." www.theparisreview.org

"Prevalence of Incontinence among Older Americans." *Vital and Health Statistics Series 3, #36*. www.cdc.gov

Price, Debora and Lynne, Livsey, 2015. "Money and Later Life." Pp. 305–312 in *Routledge Handbook of Cultural Gerontology*. Eds. Julia Twigg and Wendy Martin. New York: Routledge.

Rawcliffe, Carole, 1995. *Medicine and Society in Later Medieval Life*. London: Alan Sutton.

Rees Jones, Ian, 2015. "Connectivity, Digital Technologies, and Later Life." Pp. 439–446 in *Routledge Handbook of Cultural Gerontology*. Eds. Julia Twigg and Wendy Martin. New York: Routledge.

"Reporter Shares Life Lessons from a Year with the Oldest Old," 2018, January 25. www.NPR.org

Richardson, B.E., 1933. *Old Age among the Ancient Greeks*. New York: AMS Press.

Russell, Josiah C. 1990. "How Many of the Populations were Aged?" Pp. 119–127 in *Aging and the Aged in Medieval Europe*. Ed. Michael M. Sheehan. Toronto, Canada: Pontifical Institute of Medieval Studies.

Sandberg, Linn, 2015. "Sex, Sexuality and Later Life." Pp. 218–225 in *Routledge Handbook of Cultural Gerontology*. Eds. Julia Twigg and Wendy Martin. New York: Routledge.

Schneier, Matthew, 2016, April 17. "A 'Battle Cry' on Internet Trolling." *New York Times*: pp. 1–8.

Schwartz, Pepper, 2006. *Adventures and Advice on Sex, Love, and the Sensual Years*. New York: Harper Collins e-books.

Schwartzbaum, Lisa, 2013, September 13. "The Fear That Does Not Speak Its Name." www.nytimes.com

Segal, Lynn, 2013. *Out of Time: The Pleasures and the Perils of Ageing.* London: Verso.

"Sex in Later Life: Four Women Reveal the (Very Varied) Truth," 2014, February 24. www.dailymailco.uk

Sifferlin, Alexandra, 2016, May 31. "'Old Person Smell' Really Exists, Scientists Say." www.heathland.time

Span, Paula, 2016, October 7. "The Grey Gender Gap: Women Are Likelier to Go It Alone." www.nytimes.com

Spar, Debora L., 2016, September 24. "Aging and My Beauty Dilemma." www.newyorktimes.com

Steinem, Gloria, 2006. *Doing Sixty and Seventy.* Oakland, CA: Elders Academy Press.

———, 2015. *My Life on the Road.* New York: Random House.

Stewart, Susan, 2007. *Cosmetics and Perfume in the Roman World.* Gloucestershire: Temple.

———, 2016, January. "How Vain Were the Romans?" www.historytoday.com

Talmadge, Frank. 1990. "So Teach Us to Number Our Days: A Theology of Longevity in Jewish Exigetical Literature." Pp. 49–62 in *Aging and the Aged in Medieval Europe.* Ed. Michael M. Sheehan. Toronto, Canada: Pontifical Institute of Medieval Studies.

Tavernise, Sabrina, 2016, April 22. "U.S. Suicide Rates Surge to a 30-Year High." www.nyt.com

Telegraph Films, 2015, December 20. "Carrie Fisher Fires Back at Bodyshaming Star Wars Trolls: 'Blow Us.'" www.telegraph.co.uk

Twigg, Julia, 2015. "Dress and Age." Pp. 149–156 in *Routledge Handbook of Cultural Gerontology.* New York: Routledge.

Twigg, Julia and Wendy Martin, 2015. "The Field of Cultural Gerontology: An Introduction." Pp. 1–15 in *Routledge Handbook of Cultural Gerontology.* New York: Routledge.

Ward, Richard, 2015. "Hair and Age." Pp. 141–148 in *Routledge Handbook of Cultural Gerontology.* Eds. Julia Twigg and Wendy Martin. New York: Routledge.

Warren, Carol A.B., 1998, January 1. "Aging and Identity in Premodern Times." *Research on Aging* Vol. 20: pp. 11–35.

———, 2011. "The Eyes Have It." *Ethnography* Vol. 20: pp. 543–555.

———, 2012. "Assisted Living in 1489." *The Gerontologist* Vol. 52: pp. 698–702.

Waxman, Jayme, 2011, June 29. "From Medieval Hookers to Lady Gaga: A Brief History of the Merkin." www.laweekly.com

Weiner, Jennifer. 2016, August 26. "The Women Who Won't Wear Swimsuits." *New York Times Opinion Section.* www.nytimes.com/2016/08/26/opinion/the-women-who-wont-wear-swimsuits.html

Wertheim, Bonnie, 2016, September 29. "To Age Naturally or Not? Readers Respond to Debora L. Spar's 'Aging and Beauty Dilemma.'" www.newyorktimes.com

Williams, Kristine and Carol A.B. Warren, 2008. "Assisted Living and the Aging Trajectory." *Journal of Women and Aging* Vol. 20: pp. 309–328.

Williams, Mark, E. 2017, April 2. "Growing Old in Ancient Greece and Rome." www.psychologytoday.com

Wortley, John, 1996. "Aging in the *Patmos Floregium.*" Winnipeg, Canada: University of Manitoba. Unpublished manuscript.

Wright, Ty, 2016, October. "Donald Trump Says Accusers Are Too Ugly for Him to Have Groped." www.vanityfair.com

Ylanne, Viripi, 2015. "Representations of Ageing in the Media." Pp. 369–376 in *Routledge Handbook of Cultural Gerontology.* Eds. Julia Twigg and Wendy Martin. New York: Routledge.

Zerbi, Gabriele, [1489] 1998. *The Gerontocomia: On the Care of the Aged.* Trans. R.L. Lind. Philadelphia: American Philosophical Society.

INDEX

CPSIA information can be obtained
at www.ICGtesting.com
Printed in the USA
FSHW021254161220
76947FS